Sew Organized

for the Busy Girl

Tips to Control the Chaos & Space to Store Your Stuff + 15 Practical Projects You'll Love

Heidi Staples

stashBOOKS®

an imprint of C&T Publishing

Text copyright © 2015 by Heidi Staples

Photography and Artwork copyright © 2015 by C&T Publishing, Inc.

PUBLISHER: Amy Marson

CREATIVE DIRECTOR: Gailen Runge

ART DIRECTOR / COVER DESIGNER: Kristy Zacharias

EDITOR: Karla Menaugh

TECHNICAL EDITORS: Mary E. Flynn and Helen Frost

BOOK DESIGNER: April Mostek

COVER ILLUSTRATOR: Casey Dukes

PRODUCTION COORDINATOR: Jenny Davis

PRODUCTION EDITOR: Joanna Burgarino

ILLUSTRATOR: Aliza Shalit

PHOTO ASSISTANT: Mary Peyton Peppo

STYLED PHOTOGRAPHY by Nissa Brehmer and
INSTRUCTIONAL PHOTOGRAPHY by Diane Pedersen, unless otherwise noted

Published by Stash Books, an imprint of C&T Publishing, Inc., P.O. Box 1456, Lafayette, CA 94549

Library of Congress Cataloging-in-Publication Data

Staples, Heidi, 1977- author.

 Sew organized for the busy girl : tips to make the most of your time & space : 23 quick and clever sewing projects you'll love / by Heidi Staples.

     pages cm

ISBN 978-1-60705-979-0 (softcover)

1. Sewing. 2. House furnishings. I. Title.

TT705.S73 2015

646.2--dc23

                    2014031103

Printed in China

10 9 8 7 6 5 4 3 2 1

Table of Contents

4 DEDICATION AND ACKNOWLEDGMENTS

5 INTRODUCTION

6 WHY EVERY MODERN GIRL
SHOULD SEW

Making the Case for Sewing
My Story: How Sewing Saved My Sanity
Your Story: How This Book Can Help You

12 DESIGNING WOMAN:
Create a Space That Works for You

Discover Your Workspace Personality
Find Storage Solutions That Fit Your Space
Keep Your Work Area Clean
Stock Your Shelves to Save Time and Money
Hold Regular Fabric Auditions
Be Prepared with Project Bags
Keep a Set of Sewing Files
Surround Yourself with Inspiration

26 CALENDAR GIRL:
How to Fit Sewing into Your Schedule

You Have to Make It Happen
Use a Calendar
Kids and the Sewing Room
Know Your Limits

33 MAKE SOMETHING:
Projects and Variations

Double-Zip Clutch   34

Nine-Patch Pocket Pillows   40

Deluxe Pincushion
First Aid Station, Zippered Pouch, and Cold Pack
Book Nook

Sleepy-Time Friend Kit   50

Softie Doll • Mini Quilt
Coordinating Tote • Pillow

Baby Love Set   58

Crawl Pillow • Flutter Quilt

Chevron Table Set   64

Table Runner • Place Mats

Brass Ring Pillow   68

Envelope Clutch   72

Manicure Set • Art Pack

Jet-Set Case   78

Case • Zippered Pouch

83 MAKE SOMETHING BIGGER:
Projects for Time and Travel

Splitting a Big Project into Manageable Pieces
Traveling with Your Sewing

Summer Tourist Quilt   86

Dotty Hexagon Pillow   90

Starlet Mini Quilt   94

Girl Friday Sewing Case   98

103 JOY

105 SEWING BASICS

111 RESOURCES AND ABOUT THE AUTHOR

Dedication

To my beloved family, who not only believed that I could write a book, but also made sure that I had all the time, caffeine, and encouragement I needed to actually do it.

Acknowledgments

To Angela, Beth, Debbie, Kimberly, Lindsay, Lynne, Maureen, Sarah, and Svetlana for being kind enough to share their ideas and experience. You each deserve your own fan club.

To Karla—my editor, encourager, and all-around lifesaver. You're the best.

To the amazing team at Stash Books and C&T Publishing, who helped me make sense of the vision I had for this book. You guys are fantastic, and I am so proud to be working with you.

To all the lovely companies who donated materials so that I could write a sewing book without going broke. I (and my husband) can't thank you enough.

Author's Note

The title of this book might seem like a giant "No Boys Allowed" sign on the sewing clubhouse. Not so. While it's true that the majority of people who sew also happen to be female, and while I had plenty of fun designing these pages with that theme in mind, the principles in this book will work for you no matter what gender you happen to be. So pick up a needle, gentlemen, and let's make something…

To the many friends—online and in person—who keep me going each day with their love and laughter. I appreciate you more than I can say.

To my incredible family: Dad and Mom, David and Amy, my darling nieces, Mike and Mary, Dave and Jenna. And to Grandma, who was overjoyed about this book but didn't live to see it published. I love you all so dearly.

To Amy, who always had a listening ear and willing hands to help. You're amazing, Sis.

To my three beautiful daughters (affectionately known as Bunny, Bear & Mouse), who have been so proud of Mommy's book from the start. You are the joy of my life, and I just love you to pieces.

To my husband, James, who has been the constant voice of sanity in my life—"It doesn't have to be the best book ever written, Sweetheart, just the best book you can write." I absolutely adore you.

And to my Lord, who has brought me through doors that I never dreamed could open for me. I am so grateful. May all the glory go to You.

Introduction

I am beginning to learn that it is the sweet, simple things of life which are the real ones after all. — Laura Ingalls Wilder

There are moments when it seems as if life is spinning out of control.

I'm not talking about what you see on the nightly news. Let's not even go there. No, I'm talking about your life. When your to-do list for today takes up more than one page; when the only time you spend with your husband is falling asleep in front of the television set together; when you're perfecting the art of multitasking by learning to wash dishes, talk on the phone, and brush your daughter's hair at the same time. Insanity becomes routine, and we can't seem to remember how to slow down anymore.

Whether we like it or not, life is going to be busy … and this is not necessarily a bad thing. It becomes bad when we let the craziness hijack our lives so completely that we don't leave any room for the things that bring us joy.

We need joy. Life becomes boring and utterly depressing without it. Of course, I suspect that the names of some special people are at the top of your joy list, but could it be that sewing has made it into the top ten? If it has, then wouldn't you like to be doing it more often? Sewing just makes me happy. And when I'm happy, it's so much easier to take the petty annoyances of life in stride.

I wrote this book because I know all about living the busy life. These ideas were conceived and tested in the midst of a bustling, noisy house packed with four busy adults, three active little girls, and three completely neurotic dogs. There were days when these ideas worked to perfection and other moments when … well, not so much. Life doesn't always work out the way we plan, but I've learned that a little planning doesn't hurt.

My fondest wish is that this book will end up full of dog-eared corners, scribbled notes, and coffee stains; that it will be there for you like a personal assistant and a comfortable old friend. More than anything, I hope it will give you the chance to sew more often, and that as you do, you'll remember why you love it so much.

Let's find our way back to joy.

Why Every Modern Girl Should Sew

Why bother sewing?

You can buy clothes at Walmart for a fraction of what it costs you to make them. Home furnishings are available online at the click of a button, and styles are changing faster than anyone can keep up. Gifts line the shelves at the local mall, and if you're really desperate, you can buy something handmade (by someone else, of course) on Etsy.

Besides, who has time to sew? Have you looked at your calendar lately? Where exactly are you going to find time to do this in between meetings, errands, and the 50 other appointments on your schedule today?

Making the Case for Sewing

In today's world, it may seem as if sewing has become completely irrelevant, but I disagree. So do a lot of other people out there. The handmade revolution has exploded in recent years. There was a time when people made everything themselves because they had no other choice. Now we're choosing to make more things ourselves because we're finding that it's a more fulfilling way to live.

SEWING GIVES YOU MORE VALUE FOR YOUR MONEY. You may spend more money on a dress that you made yourself rather than one you picked up at the local chain store, but be sure you're making the right comparison: a mass-produced, cheaply made item versus a garment that has been carefully sewn and tailored to your specific measurements. How much would you spend on a dress like that if you ordered it from a dressmaker? Exactly.

SEWING SAVES YOU TIME. Dropping off clothes at the dry cleaners for small tailoring fixes, running out to find a last-minute gift—no more of that for you. You can handle all this on your own now, and often you can do it in half the time.

SEWING GIVES YOU QUALITY CONTROL. I will never forget the time I walked into an unnamed chain store in search of a tote bag to use as a gift. There were badly sewn edges, loose threads, and (quite frankly) ugly fabrics everywhere. I settled for a gift card because I was too embarrassed to give my friend the items I'd seen on the shelves. That day has stuck with me as a reminder that I don't ever need to feel like a handmade gift is a poor substitute for something from the store.

Detail of *Summer Tourist* (page 86)

SEWING LETS YOU BE CREATIVE. Remember how much fun you used to have during craft time? That need for creativity doesn't go away when you grow up. Sewing can put you back in touch with the joy of creativity, giving you the chance to make items that are both lovely and useful.

SEWING LETS YOU FINISH SOMETHING. Sewing can give you the chance to see something begin and end in a relatively short period of time. Finishing an item gives you the well-deserved sense of accomplishment.

SEWING LETS YOU SHARE THE LOVE. You can't put a price tag on love, and that's what you pour into every project that passes through your fingers. What's more meaningful—a plastic gift card or a project that someone spent hours making just for you? Hand-sewn gifts show your friends and family that they're worth more than your money … they're worth your time.

SEWING GIVES YOU THE POWER TO CHOOSE. Sewing equals freedom. We're not limited to what the style makers are offering this year. We can make exactly what we want because we're the designers of our own brand of style.

Detail of Chevron Place Mat
(page 67)

My Story: How Sewing Saved My Sanity

By fall 2011, I felt like I was about one step away from losing my mind.

Life had changed so much in the six years since my husband and I had gotten married. I had gone from being a teacher to a school administrator to a stay-at-home mom. In the midst of economic challenges, we decided to buy a large home with my parents where we could all live together—a good decision, but one that would take a few years to settle into normalcy. Our first daughter was soon joined by two more, and I was dealing with the ever-shifting joy and insanity of caring for three little girls who were just one, two, and four years old. I was happy to be where I was in life—in a frazzled, exhausted, living-on-baked-goods-and-Diet-Coke sort of way—but something was missing.

I desperately needed a hobby. All the creativity and independence of my former life seemed buried somewhere under a pile of dishes and laundry. Don't get me wrong … I was so grateful to be able to stay home with my kids, but there were days when the walls started closing in on me.

For about a year, I had bounced around from one idea to the next—picture-book writing, party planning, home fitness, interior decorating. I was interested in all of it to varying degrees, but I was passionate about none. Then one day my mom ordered a new sewing machine. When it arrived, I looked at it with a speculative eye. Was this worth trying?

I bought some fabric and supplies, asked Mom to teach me how to use the machine, and made my first mini quilt from a tutorial I found online at Purl Bee. It felt amazing to look at that finished project. I bought more fabric, added more blogs to my online reader, and tried another project … and then another. I didn't have all the techniques mastered yet, and my work was full of mistakes. For the first time, though, I didn't let that stop me, because I was having so much fun!

At the end of that December, I started my own sewing blog, Fabric Mutt, and officially joined the online quilting community. I had finally found the creative outlet I was looking for.

BUSY GIRL SPEAKS

Beth Vassalo of Plum and June (plumandjune.blogspot.com)

Why did you start blogging? I started blogging to join in the conversation and connect with other people who shared my interests.

Any advice for a new sewing blogger? Comment, comment, comment! When you see something you like, tell the person who made it. If you have a question, ask it. When people comment on your blog, respond to them. Then visit their blog and leave them a comment. Forming relationships with other bloggers is a large part of the experience, and one of the best ways to meet others is through commenting.

Your Story: How This Book Can Help You

So that's where I was. Where are you? Your challenges and responsibilities may be different, but the benefits of sewing can still make a positive difference in your life.

I'm not going to teach you how to sew. There are plenty of resources both online and in the bookstore that can bring you up to speed. What I want to show you is how to make sewing possible in the midst of your busy life. This book is for you if you are …

+ Still trying to decide if sewing is going to be worth your time.

+ A beginner who's just learning how to sew and organize your sewing space.

+ Someone who wants to sew but can't find the time to do it.

+ An experienced seamstress looking for a few new ideas to streamline the process.

Sewing gives you the tools to incorporate your own style into your handmade items.

Many modern quilters choose to start a blog. I originally started blogging so that I could share my projects with family members around the country, but it didn't take me long to branch out from there. Being a part of the online quilting community lets you communicate on a regular basis with other people around the world who love to sew as much as you do. You can quickly and easily get advice, feedback, and encouragement from friends who may even be sewing the same projects as you. I also love that my blog is a running documentation of my sewing journey. It's wonderful to look back and see how far I've come from that first quilt.

Throughout this book, keep your eyes open for tips from other busy women who have found creative ways to carve out time for sewing and blogging in their daily lives. I hope you'll feel free to make these ideas, projects, and routines completely your own. Use the Busy Girl Takes Action pages to scribble your thoughts and goals.

BUSY GIRL TAKES ACTION

1 When did you start sewing, and what made you decide to try?

_____

_____

_____

_____

2 Are your reasons for sewing now the same as they were back then?
If not, how have they changed, and why?

_____

_____

_____

3 Set a few sewing goals for the coming year!

For the first time, I want to try …

_____

_____

I'd like to get better at …

_____

_____

I don't want to worry so much about …

_____

_____

I want to get more organized with …

_____

_____

Designing Woman:
Create a Space That Works for You

Order is the shape upon which beauty depends. —Pearl S. Buck

A few years ago my family went to a nearby animal shelter to adopt a puppy. We returned home with not one but two young dogs, a brother and sister who had been more than our hearts could resist. I suddenly found myself with five children in the house—three little girls under the age of five and two furry toddlers ready for trouble. For over a year, I spent my days running from disaster to disaster: holes in the garden, cereal all over the floor, and toys in everybody's mouths. In desperation, I went to the library and checked out everything that offered advice on child rearing and dog training. In the end, all the books said essentially the same thing: it's not so much about training *them* as it is about training *you* to know how to help them.

I've learned that the same advice applies to a lot of things in life—yes, even your sewing room. What matters isn't the setup; it's all about what you do with it.

Some people have perfectly decorated studios that are always a mess, while others can keep a lovely sewing corner with hardly more than a set of plastic boxes. You are the biggest factor in how organized your space is going to be and how efficiently it's going to work for you. It involves a bit of training, of course, and a whole lot of practice. But when you have a handle on what works for you and what fits your style, it all comes together to make a place where you love to sew.

Photo by Heidi Staples

Storing fabric so you can see each piece at a glance lets you focus on creativity, rather than on searching for the perfect orange you think you bought last month.

DISCOVER YOUR WORKSPACE PERSONALITY

To figure out how you need to organize your sewing space, take a few minutes to figure out yourself. Going through these questions will help you understand what works best for you in your sewing space.

1 It's easiest for me to choose fabrics for a project when I look at them …

A. By color.

B. By collection.

C. By style (geometric, floral, solid, novelty, and so forth).

D. By designer.

E. By _____.

2 My level of sewing room cleanliness is …

A. Touch my stuff and die.

B. A place for everything and everything in its place.

C. I'll clean up when I'm done working … probably.

D. I know which pile everything is in.

E. Where's my sewing machine?

F. Jekyll & Hyde—I go back and forth between_____ and _____.

3 When I need something, it should be …

A. Within arm's reach.

B. No more than a few steps away.

C. In the same room where I'm working.

D. Somewhere in the house—I don't mind having to leave the room a few times in an hour for certain materials.

4 I want my sewing room to be …

A. Matchy-matchy—I love it when everything goes together!

B. Retro—Vintage style makes me swoon!

C. Eclectic—My inspiration comes from everywhere, so why shouldn't my decor?

D. Modern—Clean lines and bold design always fuel my creativity!

E. Practical—We're here to sew, not decorate. Bring on the fabric!

F. A combination of_____.

G. Something totally different—My style is _____.

Find Storage Solutions That Fit Your Space

Whether you're setting up your sewing room for the very first time or your workspace really needs a complete overhaul, you need to follow just a few simple steps to start out with a clean slate.

1. HIT THE RESET BUTTON.

The most efficient and effective way to really clean a room is to take everything out of it and start over. Pull everything off the shelves and out of the drawers, putting it in boxes or even in a pile on the floor.

Take a look at the storage units you've been using. If anything (a) is broken beyond repair, (b) isn't a good fit for your stuff, or (c) makes you sick to look at it anymore (Yes, I've been there too!), then it doesn't belong in your space. Throw it out or give it away. Take a few minutes to clean up the storage that's left. Make a note if you need extra containers or storage units.

Take a look at the room layout. Keep in mind how you work. Do you need a spot where you can gather all your materials before you start working because some of your storage is in another room? Do you work well in a small space, or do you need room to spread out everything? Do you have a design wall, or will you need a table or open floor space for arranging quilt blocks? Make a sketch or two before you start moving furniture and hanging things on the wall.

Photo by Heidi Staples

Take a few minutes to sketch out a room layout before you start moving furniture.

LET'S TALK ABOUT ... STORAGE

You need a place to put your stuff, and that usually means one of three things: shelves, drawers, or containers. Any of these will work as long as they're big enough for what you have with a little extra room to grow. My storage includes an antique secretary desk, a wire mesh cart, a modern shelving unit, a wooden unit with plastic drawers, an antique cupboard, tin buckets, wire mesh buckets, and glass canning jars.

It probably sounds as if I must occupy an entire floor of our house to have enough room for all this, but actually my sewing space is about seven feet by twelve feet, taking up less than half of a room that also serves as my office and a classroom for one of my daughters. My space also contains our old kitchen sideboard and a large sewing table that was formerly my dad's office desk

I share this with you because I want you to be open-minded when it comes to storage. I have a crazy mix of furniture and containers that don't actually go together but still manage to work perfectly for my space. Using items that are almost all recycled or repurposed appeals to me too, and not just because I'm trying to be environmentally responsible. I love the vintage, eclectic feel that it gives to my workspace. I also like using storage units that can be easily picked up and moved, so a lot of my sewing items are in containers with handles. Think outside the box when you start to explore what you want to use for storage.

A variety of household items, like baskets, jars, or even coffee mugs, can serve as storage pieces in your sewing area.

2. GO THROUGH EVERYTHING.

And, yes, I mean everything. This is where you again will need to be brutally honest with yourself. If an item gets a spot on your shelf, it has to earn its keep. That bolt of fabric may have been marked down to 90 percent off the original price, but if you don't like it anymore, why are you letting it steal space from fabric that you love? If you have kept every issue of a quilting magazine for the past five years, it may be time to snap pictures of your favorite pages and free up room on your bookshelf.

If you can't use an item, don't like it, or just don't want to have to store it anymore, get rid of it. This doesn't mean you have to throw it away. Give it to a friend who's just starting out, see if a local sewing class might be able to use it, or sell it online to someone who will be thrilled to give it a new home. I know that this step can be draining and even downright painful, but it's crucial to the organization of your workspace.

It helps to have three staging areas: keep, donate, and trash. I recommend using big black trash bags for the last two categories. It's a little easier to let things go when you don't have to see them again and they're already packed to go to their next destination. Try to go through all of your items at one sitting or at least in one day. It's better to get this part over quickly when you're in the right mind-set to do it.

LET'S TALK ABOUT ... SCRAPS

Scraps are such a personal topic. While I love a good scrappy project, I find it almost impossible to keep up with the contents of my scrap bins, and this can lead to major sewing guilt. After all, shouldn't I be making use of every last bit of my beautiful fabric?

Don't let guilt creep into your sewing room. If you can't use the scraps, you can't use them. Give them away or sell them. If you can't, it's okay—it really is—to throw away pieces that aren't going to be used. I promise, I won't tell a soul.

Photo by Heidi Staples

Scraps—do you love to use them, or do they overtake your sewing area?

3. CHOOSE A SYSTEM.

It doesn't matter what system you use to organize your sewing supplies. The important thing is that you have one. I keep some fabric collections together, especially if I plan to use them together in a project. Most of my fabric, though, is organized by color. This helps me be spontaneous as I mix up prints, and it also helps me find what I'm looking for pretty quickly.

How to physically store your fabric is also your call. Some people make miniature bolts of cloth by wrapping fabric around small pieces of cardboard, while others just fold and stack. Some people even roll up pieces of fabric and drop them in a drawer. What matters for you is that you can quickly find and use what you need when you need it. Find a designated home for each of the following:

+ Large lengths of fabric (several yards or more)

+ Medium lengths of fabric (between a yard and a fat quarter)

+ Small lengths of fabric (less than a fat quarter but bigger than a scrap)

+ Scraps (We'll leave this definition up to you.)

+ Special types of fabric (linen, voile, and laminates, for example)

Photo by Heidi Staples

Keep similar items together so you can keep track of your inventory.

The same idea applies to your tools and notions. Try to set aside containers, shelves, or drawers with similar items together. This may sound like common sense, but it's all too easy to end up with supplies everywhere when you're working on one project after another. Before you know it, you have to check five places to find the items you need or, even worse, go out to buy more only to discover that you already had the items buried under a stack in the corner. You just don't need these problems, especially when your sewing time is limited.

When the last piece of fabric has been stored away and the last box of notions is emptied, take a seat and look over your kingdom. You've worked hard to make this room a beautiful place. Now let's talk about how to keep it that way.

EASIEST SEWING ROOM STORAGE IDEA EVER

Grab a picnic utensil holder and fill it with a few books, sewing notions, and some fabric. This household item works well for

Photo by Heidi Staples

corralling the tools you're using most at the moment so that you don't have everything laying out on the table—especially helpful if you have a tiny sewing space. And if you want to sew in another room or even outside, just grab this kit by the handle and take it all with you.

Keep Your Work Area Clean

It really helps when everything in your workspace has its own spot and returns to that spot when you finish sewing for the day. I used to spend at least a quarter of my time trying to find things—bad news when I had so little sewing time. There are still days when I have to leave my sewing room in a mess because it just can't be helped, but even then I take at least a minute to put all my cutting tools back in their jars and put the iron away. Frankly, this is also a safety issue in my house. The last thing I want is to leave something dangerous out where one of my little girls will surely find it.

It's a good idea to do an official Clean Sweep every now and then. A few months back I bought myself a cute timer to use for this sort of thing. I just set the timer for ten, fifteen, or twenty minutes—depending on how much of an overachiever I feel like that day—and then I clean until the bell rings. It's incredible how much I can get done in such a short amount of time. Once in a while I even keep cleaning past the time limit. If you can do a Clean Sweep at least once a week, you'll probably be in good shape.

Does this mean that I have a pristine showplace for a sewing room? Of course not. As I type this sentence, I'm trying not to feel guilt over the heaps I left behind on my sewing table this morning. The difference is that I don't plan to leave it that way. This weekend I'll pull out my timer, restore order, and get my routines back in place again.

Photo by Heidi Staples

A Clean Sweep can put your sewing area back in shape.

Stock Your Shelves to Save Time and Money

I used to decide what I was going to make and then go out to buy supplies. I was on my way to the fabric store to buy interfacing for the second time one week when my husband said, "If you know you're going to be using this stuff all the time, why don't you just buy a lot of it so you don't have to keep running to the store?"

I suddenly realized how many of these basic items I was constantly purchasing in small amounts and how much I could save in gas money, shipping, and time by buying in bulk less frequently. Having items on hand also makes it possible for me to whip up a project immediately instead of waiting until I can get supplies. See Sewing Basics (pages 105–110) for information about supplies I keep on hand.

Photo by Heidi Staples

Keep a shopping list just for sewing supplies.

Hold Regular Fabric Auditions

My favorite part of the sewing process is designing a new project. I love the thrill of figuring out a new pattern and choosing just the right fabrics. The problem is that I'm not satisfied until I get the fabrics exactly right, and that can sometimes take more time than I have available. One habit that has really helped me is holding weekly fabric auditions.

A fabric audition is simply a way to practice pulling fabrics that fit a specific theme. Once I have a stack that I like, I give it a name and take a few pictures of it in different positions (usually one with the prints all fanned out and one of the stack from the side). Then I put the fabrics back on the shelf.

This gives me (a) great practice at putting together fabric combinations and (b) a resource file of possibilities for future projects. I use some of my auditioned fabrics immediately and some never. But when I'm in a hurry, I know where to find ideas that work. I store all my fabric audition photos in a special file on my computer, so I can pull them up whenever I'm looking for inspiration.

THE ANATOMY OF A FABRIC AUDITION

I'm looking for some candy colors today. Red, aqua, and pink are calling my name, but I also want to throw in a touch of black to ground the mix. I quickly start pulling fabrics until I have a nice group of prints to look at more closely.

Overall, I like the range of prints. There are saturated colors and slightly low-volume choices. Small, medium, and large prints are represented, as well as floral, geometric, and even a few text options.

In the end, I remove only three of my original choices. The leaf print is a great shade of red, but the lines are brown instead of the black that I'm looking for. I love the herringbone design, yet I'm afraid it has too much of a purple tone. And while I adore the strawberry print, the colors feel just a little off from the rest of the audition. I'm left with twelve great fabrics that will play nicely together in whatever project I decide to make.

A variety of candy colors

After removing three prints, I have twelve fabrics that go well together.

Be Prepared with Project Bags

To help me stay ready to sew in a hurry, I keep project bags on hand. When I want to make a project for a special event or when I have an idea but not enough time to start sewing, I put together one of these little beauties.

A project bag can keep all your supplies together, ready to pick up and use whenever you have a few minutes to sew.

Project bags require only a few simple items:

+ Gallon-size plastic bags

+ Project bag forms

+ The materials you need to make the item

+ A container in which you'll keep the bags

Let's say that I want to make a zippered pencil pouch for my niece's birthday. First I'll gather the materials: fabrics and interfacing (both of which I can precut right now if I have the time), a matching zipper, and maybe some twill tape for a key-ring loop. Next I'll take a minute to fill out a project bag form to remind me what occasion this project is for, whether I need to add any materials, and the pattern name. I put the form and the materials into the bag, zip it closed, and drop it in the storage container. Ta-daaa! I am now a super-prepared, incredibly organized woman!

The next time I walk into my sewing room without an immediate project in mind or I have a few extra minutes left at the end of a sewing session, I can open one of those bags and get started quickly. It doesn't get more efficient than that.

Photo by Heidi Staples

Keep your project bags in an easily accessible place.

PROJECT BAG SHEETS

Making your own project bag sheets is a snap. Underneath the title, just list these five items with a blank line or two after each one: project name, occasion, pattern, missing pieces, and notes.

Copy and paste another set of text below the first, and you can fit two forms on one sheet of paper. Or make it really easy on yourself and download a ready-made form on my blog, fabricmutt.blogspot.com.

Keep a Set of Sewing Files

One of my best decisions was to start a set of sewing files. I was having a dreadful time keeping track of pattern pieces, sketches, and photocopies from sewing books. I finally bought a set of plain manila file folders and designated each one for a different sewing book or pattern. I also file graph paper and finished sketches.

Instead of conventional file labels, I use decorative tape and a permanent marker to label my files. The tape looks pretty and can be changed easily. A rectangular wire mesh basket makes the perfect spot for these files, keeping them out where I can see them and easily grab something whenever I need it.

I also keep business cards for fabric shops, addresses for sewing-swap partners, and brochures from fabric companies in a file folder. And I keep an address book just for sewing-related contacts. It's up to you if you prefer keeping that information on paper, on a tech device, or on both.

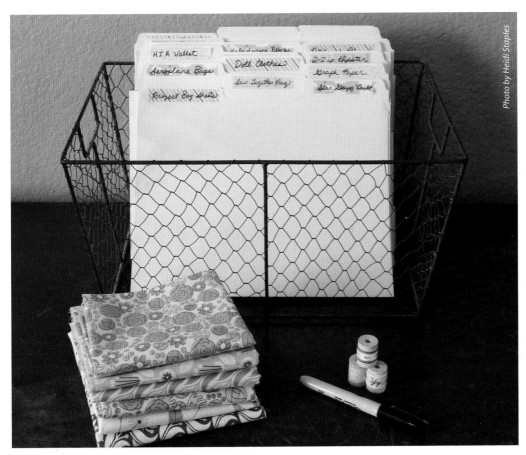

Photo by Heidi Staples

A wire mesh basket keeps my sewing files corralled.

Surround Yourself with Inspiration

One of the best things you can add to your sewing space is an inspiration board. This can be a bulletin board, a magnetic chalkboard, even a few rows of twine pinned on the wall with a set of clothespins for hanging things. Fill it with items that make you happy: swatches of your favorite fabrics, old postcards, photos of your latest vacation, pictures from magazines. If you have room, decorate your space with accents like lamps, pillows, bookends, plants, framed pictures, and mini quilts to bring more of your personality to the room and make it a place where you always feel at home.

Photo by Heidi Staples

Fill an inspiration board with items that make you happy.

BUSY GIRL TAKES ACTION

1 Sketch some ideas for your sewing space, including a floor plan and storage options. Don't make this plan an unreachable ideal. It should be one that you can actually create within your workspace.

2 Schedule time for a sewing room makeover, when you can go through the three organizational steps we talked about in Find Storage Solutions That Fit Your Space (page 15). If you think you can't do it alone, bring in a friend or family member.

3 Try putting together at least one fabric audition or project bag per week. Do you have any ideas for these already? Write them down here to get you started.

4 Set up your own sewing files. If this looks like it's going to be a massive project, work on it ten minutes each night for a week or until it's done.

5 Create an inspiration board for your sewing room and bring some new decorative objects into your workspace. If you already have these in place, mix it up a little by removing a few old items and adding some new favorites.

Calendar Girl:

How to Fit Sewing into Your Schedule

People often ask me how I find time to do everything I do. Between cleaning, cooking, homeschooling my daughters, and running errands each week, where do I find the time to sew and blog?

You Have to Make It Happen

For me, sewing is not always a tidy process. Let's take a look at a little piece of my day …

Noon: Put Mouse down for a nap, start playtime for Bear, get Bunny started on afternoon schoolwork.

12:15 p.m.: Sit down at my workspace to start sewing.

12:23 p.m.: Stop to put Mouse back in bed after she stages a protest.

12:36 p.m.: Start pressing the fabric I need for a project.

12:45 p.m.: Stop to answer the phone; remind the local newspaper for the 257th time that we really are not interested in a subscription.

12:52 p.m.: Get back to my pressing.

12:56 p.m.: Stop to help Bunny with the mysteries of bar graphs.

1:07 p.m.: Finish pressing and start cutting my fabric.

1:20 p.m.: Mouse wakes up; stop to get her settled in the family room with Bear.

1:26 p.m.: Back to the sewing table … what was I doing again?

Yes, it's true. My daily sewing takes place in ridiculously random fits and starts.

If I waited to sew until I had an uninterrupted stretch of time, I wouldn't sew nearly as often. But it's also important for me to schedule chunks of sewing time so I can focus on my work and let someone else hold down the fort. To do that, I have a little weekly habit that makes it work.

Use a Calendar

Every Sunday after church, my family goes out for lunch together, and one of the many things we talk about is the week ahead. We go over any activities for the next seven days, including standing appointments, special events, and family meals. Once the big items are scheduled, we see where we can plug in a few blocks of gardening time for my husband and sewing time for me.

I highly recommend that you have a planning session like this with your family on a regular basis and that your sewing time is a standing topic on the agenda. We're used to scheduling time for work or for our children's activities. But if sewing is an important part of your life, it deserves a place in your schedule as well.

For our family, this conversation works best on a weekly basis. You know your situation well enough to decide whether this should be a weekly or monthly meeting with your loved ones.

Sewing time isn't the only thing that belongs on your calendar. I find it extremely helpful to also keep track of any occasions requiring hand-sewn gifts. Birthdays, weddings, and baby showers are all great opportunities to make something personal for the people you love.

If you're active online, you should note special events in the blogging community. Blog-hop posts, swap-package shipping dates, and special blog linkups can slip by unnoticed if you don't record them on your calendar.

Photo by Heidi Staples

Keeping a calendar helps you create time for sewing in your busy lifestyle.

Detail of *Weekend Tourist* (page 89)

Come up with your own system for marking dates. Use symbols, pen colors, highlighters, or stickers to mark each type of reminder. This will help you know, at a glance, what you're looking at. It's up to you if you want to make these notes a part of your regular calendar or if you want to keep a separate planner just for sewing.

I also find it very helpful to set weekly goals for my sewing projects. If I know that I have eight items that need to be done this month, it takes me just a few minutes to assign two projects per week on my calendar. I know that if I stick with it, I won't be facing a pile of work crammed into the last few days of the month.

There's nothing fancy about this calendar system, but habits like this can make all the difference when it comes to your stress level. If everyone in your family has an idea of how much time is going to be devoted to hobbies and how much time is reserved for family, the guesswork goes out of the equation, and a lot of frustration goes out the back door.

BUSY GIRL SPEAKS

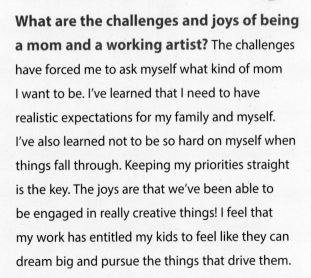

Sarah Jane Wright of
Sarah Jane Studios
(sarahjanestudios.com/blog)

What are the challenges and joys of being a mom and a working artist? The challenges have forced me to ask myself what kind of mom I want to be. I've learned that I need to have realistic expectations for my family and myself. I've also learned not to be so hard on myself when things fall through. Keeping my priorities straight is the key. The joys are that we've been able to be engaged in really creative things! I feel that my work has entitled my kids to feel like they can dream big and pursue the things that drive them.

Kids and the Sewing Room

For many of us, the people in our life are little people. Kids and sewing can be a tough mix, especially when kids are young. Sewing rooms are full of all things sharp, heavy, and hot—everything we tell them to avoid at all costs—so it can be difficult to know how to keep everyone safe when children are underfoot.

Some mothers fence off a portion of the room, some keep everything open, and others make it all off-limits. If you don't feel comfortable having your kids in the room, then go with the feeling. There will be time later to revisit your decision as they grow up.

If you decide that you want your kids in the room, you have the dilemma of how to keep them occupied while you're busy. Here are just a few ideas…

+ Keep a box of toys and books that can be played with only in the sewing room.

+ Find a way to let them help you. For instance, my daughters love to pass me Clover clips as I need them.

+ Let them play "fabric shop," using remnants that are just for play or some of your own fabric.

+ Let them sort scraps into color bins. My daughters love doing this, and it's a great teaching tool for both colors and sorting.

Photo by Heidi Staples

+ Let them design a project of their own by drawing a sketch, choosing fabric, and (when you have time to help them) sewing it together. Remember that even little ones can sew by sitting in your lap and placing one or both of their hands on top of yours as you guide fabric through the machine.

+ Let them use a sketchbook and coloring materials to design their own fabric collection. You can even have one or more designs printed through a source like Spoonflower to use in a special project. (See Resources, page 111.)

Sleepy-Time
Friend Kit
(page 50)

Know Your Limits

Blog hops, sew alongs, gifts for family and friends—pretty soon I end up with a hundred things on my to-do list and no time left for the people I love. If you also find yourself occasionally veering toward overachiever territory, it's a good idea to think about where your boundaries need to be. Here are a few of my personal guidelines:

+ No joining more than one swap at a time and only if my other obligations are fairly light.

+ No hosting blogging events unless I can clear my calendar of almost everything else during that time.

+ Maintain an average of one to three blog posts per week. I don't need to feel pressure to post every day.

+ If the girls need me—to help, to listen, to hug— sewing stops. Period.

+ Join sewing events only for projects I love.

+ Unless there is a serious deadline looming, the laptop stays downstairs at night; evenings are for my family—not for work.

Make your list of boundaries and stick to them. Sewing time should be happy time … no guilt allowed.

BUSY GIRL TAKES ACTION

1 Use a sewing calendar to come up with your own system for tracking sewing time, occasions, and events.

2 Take a look at the next month on your calendar. What do you want or need to finish this month? Break down your goals or assignments by writing down one or two per week.

3 Decide on the policy for your sewing room—kid-friendly or kid-free zone? Brainstorm a few ideas for entertaining the troops when you're busy.

_____

_____

_____

_____

_____

4 Take a few minutes to think about your own set of sewing boundaries. What are your priorities? What are the lines you don't want to cross?

_____

_____

_____

_____

_____

Make Something

Projects and Variations

I dwell in possibility. —Emily Dickinson

When I'm in the biggest hurry to finish sewing projects, it's usually because I'm trying to sew up a last-minute gift: a teacher's birthday, a baby shower for one of my husband's coworkers, presents for family members. These are the times when I'm most desperate for a project that is both quick to make and easy to personalize. The projects in this chapter were created specifically for those types of quick-deadline situations.

Some of the projects are part of a set. You can make one piece or the whole collection. Other projects show variations on a single pattern. By making something bigger, smaller, or with a few extras, you can create an item to fit your special occasion.

Remember that these patterns are only a place to start. Add patchwork details, extra pockets, and fancy pleats, or go the other way and make a more intricate project into something a little simpler. And enjoy yourself. Because after all, if it isn't any fun, it's not a hobby anymore … it's just work.

Double-Zip Clutch

CLUTCH SIZE:

11″ × 8½″ closed,
11″ × 17″ open

This project is probably the most adaptable one in the book. Adjust the size, fabric choices, and inner pocket formation to make a gift that will fit just about any situation. See Bright Idea! (page 39).

FABRIC REQUIREMENTS AND CUTTING INSTRUCTIONS

	FABRIC:	FOR:	CUTTING:
☐	½ yard floral print	Exterior	Cut 2 rectangles 12″ × 18″.
☐	Fat quarter gray polka dot print	Inside pockets	Cut 1 rectangle 12″ × 16″.
☐	½ yard black-and-white print	Flap	Cut 2 rectangles 4″ × 8″.
		Zippered pocket lining	Cut 4 rectangles 7″ × 12″.
☐	1¾ yards interfacing, 20″ width (I used Pellon Craft-Fuse.)	Exterior	Cut 2 rectangles 12″ × 18″.
		Zippered pocket lining	Cut 4 rectangles 7″ × 12″.
		Inside pockets	Cut 1 rectangle 7¾″ × 12″.
		Flap	Cut 2 rectangles 4″ × 8″.
☐	Findings: 3″ strip of ¾″ hook-and-loop tape OR 1 magnetic closure; 2 zippers, 12″ or longer		

Double-Zip Clutch

opens to 11″ × 17″ to hold stationery or other items

Making the Clutch

Seam allowances are ¼″ unless otherwise noted.

INSIDE POCKETS

Fuse interfacing to the wrong side of the fabrics for the exterior, inner pocket, and flap. See Supplies (page 105).

1 Right sides together, fold the inner pocket fabric in half to make a rectangle 12″ × 8″. Stitch the raw edges together along the 12″ side.

2 Fuse the 7¾″ × 12″ interfacing rectangle to one side of the inner pocket unit. Turn the unit right side out. Press. Topstitch ¼″ from the edge of each 12″ side.

Add interfacing, turn the unit right side out, press, and topstitch.

3 Center the inner pocket unit from Step 2 on the right side of one of the exterior pieces. Baste the short ends of the inner pocket in place.

4 Sew down the center of the inner pocket, backstitching at both ends, to make 2 wide pockets. To add extra slots in the wide pockets, stitch from the 12″ side of the inner pocket toward the center seam, backstitching at both ends.

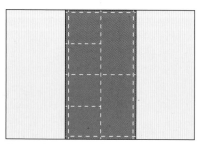

Center the inner pocket unit on the right side of an exterior piece. Stitch to create custom pockets.

FLAP

1 If you are using a magnetic closure, follow the product instructions to install half of the magnetic closure centered 1″ from a short end of a flap rectangle.

2 Right sides together, pair the flap rectangles and machine stitch ¼″ from the edge all the way around, leaving a few inches open on a long side for turning. Trim the corners at an angle.

3 Turn the flap right side out. Push out the corners with a turning tool. Tuck the raw edges of the opening inside the flap and machine stitch ⅛″ from the edge all around the flap, stitching the opening closed.

4 If you are using a hook-and-loop tape closure, center half of the strip about ½″ from a short end of the flap. Topstitch around the perimeter of the strip, just inside the edge.

Center hook-and-loop tape ½″ from the flap's short end.

5 Place the exterior rectangle that does not have the inner pocket sewn to it faceup on the work surface. Center the flap's short end (the end that does not contain the closure) on top of a short end of the exterior rectangle, overlapping the 2 pieces by about 1¼″.

Pin or clip the flap in place and machine stitch a ½″ × 3″ rectangle along the short end of the flap to secure the flap to the exterior.

6 Center the other half of the magnetic closure or hook-and-loop tape on top of the opposite end of the exterior rectangle, about 5″ from the edge. Attach it in place just as you did the first half of the closure. Before moving to the next step, fold this exterior piece and close the flap to make sure that everything is lined up correctly.

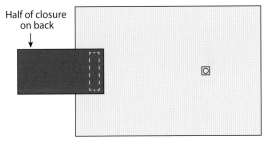

Half of closure on back

Center the flap on one end of the exterior fabric and the other half of the closure (snap shown) about 5″ from the opposite end.

ZIPPERED POCKET LININGS

1 Stack in this order from bottom to top, aligning and stitching along a 12″ side:

+ Exterior piece with inner pockets, right side up

+ Zipper, right side down, with the zipper closed

+ One of the zippered pocket lining pieces, right side down

Sew close to the zipper teeth. Keep the zipper pull out of the way while you sew. Press the fabric away from the zipper.

NOTE: *Many people switch to a zipper foot on their machine to do this step. I have no problem using my regular sewing foot. Do what works for you.*

2 Repeat Step 1 on the other side of the zipper, but stack from bottom to top:

+ Exterior piece with flap, right side up

+ Zipper, right side down

+ Another zippered pocket lining piece, right side down

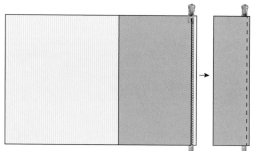

Sew each side of the zipper between one end of an exterior piece and a zippered pocket lining piece.

3 Repeat Steps 1 and 2 to attach the other zipper and remaining 2 zippered pocket lining pieces to the opposite ends of the exterior pieces. Keep the first zippered pocket lining and flap pieces out of the way while you sew the second end pocket in place. Be sure to orient the zipper so both zippers will open and close in the same direction.

CLUTCH ASSEMBLY

1 Unzip both zippers at least halfway. Arrange the unit so the exterior pieces are right sides together, with exterior pieces in the center and the pocket linings extending out on both sides. Clip or pin all the way around. As you pin, finger-press the zipper teeth toward the exterior pieces.

Leave open.

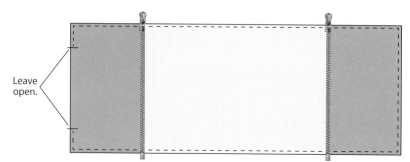

Pin or clip the clutch halves together and stitch around the perimeter, leaving an edge open for turning.

2 Sew ¼″ from the edge all the way around the bag, leaving an opening on the 12″ edge of one end pocket for turning and backstitching at the start and finish. Trim the corners so that they turn easily.

3 Turn the clutch right side out. Push out all corners with a chopstick or turning tool. Press.

4 Tuck in the raw edges of the end pocket and press. Topstitch just along the edge of the opening, backstitching at both ends.

5 Push the linings of both end pockets inside the clutch. Press again. Fold the bag so the inner pockets are inside and the flap closes neatly.

 **Bright Idea!**

If you need a last-minute gift, this is the pattern to use. It's a quick finish and adaptable to so many different gift ideas. Here are just a few gift pack themes, with ideas for what to tuck inside:

+ Toy car garage: toy cars, racing mat, miniature orange cones

+ Game night pouch: travel, handheld, and card games

+ Kitchen set: recipe cards, pencils, measuring spoons, equivalency chart, and grocery list notepad

+ Beauty kit: nail polish, makeup, face wipes, lotion, brushes, and mirror compact

+ Wedding day emergency kit: mints, double-sided tape, safety pins, bobby pins, and facial tissue

+ Diaper pack (page 63): wipes, tissues, cream, and hand sanitizer

+ Doll wardrobe: doll (handmade or purchased), clothes, and accessories

+ Puzzle pouch: jigsaw puzzles (one in each zippered pouch) or puzzle books and pencils

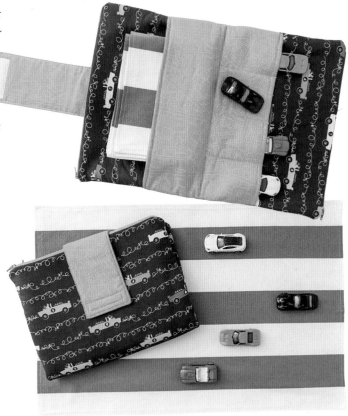

This kid-friendly version of the Double-Zip Clutch could hold toy cars or games and puzzles. I hemmed some striped canvas to make a racing mat and added some cars for this kit.

Nine-Patch Pocket Pillows

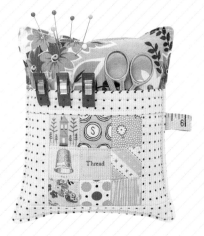

DELUXE PINCUSHION SIZE:

5½″ × 6½″ with 4½″ pocket

FIRST AID STATION SIZE:

16″ × 16″ with 10″ pocket, plus 5¾″ × 4½″ zippered pouch and 6½″ × 5″ cold pack

This is a fairly simple project, but oh, the possibilities when you change the size and add a few accessories! Use similar construction methods but vary the size to make a pincushion, first aid station, or library cushion. A variety of Nine-Patch blocks enhance each project.

BOOK NOOK SIZE:

26″ × 26″ with 20″ pocket

Deluxe Pincushion

5½″ × 6½″ with 4½″ pocket

Make your pincushion work overtime by adding a pocket for embroidery scissors and sewing clips. A miniature Nine-Patch block is a great way to show off your favorite tiny prints.

FABRIC REQUIREMENTS AND CUTTING INSTRUCTIONS

	FABRIC:	FOR:	CUTTING:
❏	9 scraps at least 1½″ square	Nine-Patch block	From each of 9 prints, cut 1 square 1½″ × 1½″.
❏	¼ yard white polka-dot print	Nine-Patch border	Cut 2 rectangles 1¾″ × 3½″. Cut 2 rectangles 1¼″ × 6″.
		Pocket lining	Cut 1 rectangle 5″ × 6″.
❏	¼ yard floral print	Pincushion body	Cut 2 rectangles 6″ × 7″.
❏	⅛ yard batting	Pocket	Cut 1 rectangle 4½″ × 6″.
❏	Twill tape or ribbon	Side loop	Cut 1 piece 3″ long.
❏	Polyester stuffing		

Making the Pincushion

Seam allowances are ¼″ unless otherwise noted.

NINE-PATCH POCKET

1 Arrange the 1½″ squares into a 3 × 3 grid. Sew together to make a Nine-Patch block.

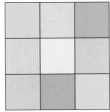

Sew squares together in a 3 × 3 grid.

2 Sew the 1¾″ × 3½″ borders to opposite sides of the Nine-Patch block. Sew the 1¼″ × 6½″ borders to the top and bottom.

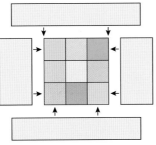

Add borders to the sides first and then to the top and bottom.

3 Right sides together, pair the Nine-Patch unit and the pocket lining rectangle. Sew together along the top edge.

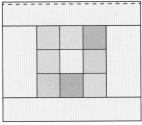

Topstitch ¼″ from the pocket's upper edge.

Fold the unit so the wrong sides are together and slip the batting inside. Press. Topstitch ¼″ from the seamed edge. Quilt the patchwork as desired.

4 Right sides up, place the pocket at the bottom edge of a pincushion body rectangle, aligning the raw edges. Baste in place.

SIDE LOOP

Fold the twill tape in half, wrong sides together and matching short ends. Stitch together ⅛″ from the raw edges. Align the raw edges of the tape with the right side of the pocket just below the topstitching. Baste in place.

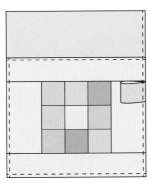

Baste the pocket and loop to the pincushion top.

PINCUSHION ASSEMBLY

1 Right sides together, pair the pincushion body pieces. Sew around the perimeter, leaving a 4″–5″ gap at the top. Trim the corners at an angle. Turn right side out, pushing out the corners with a turning tool. Press.

2 Stuff the pincushion. Tuck the open edges into the gap at the top. Topstitch ⅛″ from the edge all around the pincushion.

First Aid Station

The First Aid Station includes a zippered pouch and cold pack.

This pillow corrals some supplies for your next first aid emergency. A detachable zippered pouch holds medicine and bandages. A cold pack can go from the freezer to the pillow's pocket, where it can become a resting spot for the injured party. Pink, white, and black prints turn a simple Nine-Patch block into a clever take on an internationally recognized emergency medical symbol.

FABRIC REQUIREMENTS AND CUTTING INSTRUCTIONS

	FABRIC:	FOR:	CUTTING:
❑	20 pink-and-white print scraps at least 2″ square	Nine-Patch block	From each of 20 prints, cut 1 square 2″ × 2″.
❑	Fat quarter or ¼ yard black sketchy print	Nine-Patch block corners	Cut 4 squares 3½″ × 3½″.
		Nine-Patch border	Cut 2 rectangles 4″ × 9½″.
			Cut 2 rectangles 1″ × 16½″.
❑	Fat quarter pink floral print	Pocket lining	Cut 1 rectangle 10½″ × 16½″.
❑	⅓ yard batting	Pocket	Cut 1 rectangle 9½″ × 16½″.
❑	½ yard white-and-black geometric print	Pillow body	Cut 1 square 16½″ × 16½″.
❑	½ yard pink-and-white dash print	Pillow backing	Cut 2 rectangles 13″ × 16½″.
❑	⅛ yard dark pink dotted print	Pillow loop	Cut 1 rectangle 3″ × 4″.
		Pouch strap	Cut 1 rectangle 4″ × 6″.
❑	¼ yard green-and-pink floral print	Zippered pouch exterior	Cut 2 rectangles 6¼″ × 5″.
❑	¼ yard light pink dotted print	Zippered pouch lining	Cut 2 rectangles 6¼″ × 5″.
❑	¼ yard green novelty print	Cold pack exterior	Cut 2 rectangles 7″ × 5½″.
❑	¼ yard muslin	Cold pack interior	Cut 2 rectangles 6″ × 4½″.
❑	Findings: 1 D-ring, 1″ long; 1 swiveling lobster clasp, 1″ long; 1 zipper, 7″ or longer; rice; 16″ × 16″ pillow form		

Making the Pillow

Seam allowances are ¼″ unless otherwise noted.

First Aid Pillow, 16″ × 16″ with 10″ pocket

NINE-PATCH POCKET

1 Arrange the pink-and-white 2″ squares into 2 × 2 grids. Make 5 sets. Sew each set together to make a four-patch unit.

Four-patch unit—Make 5.

2 Arrange the Nine-Patch block corner squares and the units from Step 1 in a 3 × 3 grid. Sew together to make a Nine-Patch block.

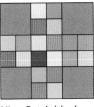

Nine-Patch block— Make 1.

3 Sew the 4″ × 9½″ borders to opposite sides of the Nine-Patch block. Sew the 1″ × 16½″ borders to the top and bottom.

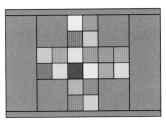

Add borders to the sides first and then to the top and bottom.

4 Right sides together, pair the Nine-Patch block and the pocket lining rectangle. Stitch together along the top edge.

Fold the unit so wrong sides are together and slip the batting inside. Press. Topstitch ¼″ from the seamed edge. Quilt the patchwork as desired.

5 Right sides up, place the pocket at the bottom edge of the pillow top square, aligning the raw edges. Baste in place.

SIDE LOOP

1 Fold the loop rectangle in half to make a strip 2″ × 3″. Press. Open and fold the 4″ edges in to meet at the center fold. Press. Fold again at the original line, sandwiching the raw edges inside the strip, to make a 1″ × 3″ strip.

Topstitch about ⅛″ from the edge of each 3″ side. Fold the loop in half, raw edges together. Thread the D-ring into the loop and stitch ⅛″ from the short raw edges to secure.

Fold the long edges toward the center of the strip and topstitch. Add a D-ring.

2 Align the raw edges of the loop with the right side of the pillow/pocket unit, about 7″ from the upper edge. Baste in place.

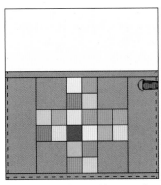

Baste the pocket and loop to the pillow top.

PILLOW ASSEMBLY

1 On each pillow backing rectangle, fold under ½˝ along a 16½˝ edge. Press. Fold under another ½˝. Press. Topstitch ¼˝ and ½˝ from the fold.

2 Make a stack in this order from bottom to top:

+ Pillow top, right side up

+ Pillow backing piece with raw edges aligned with the upper half of the pillow top, right side down

+ Pillow backing piece with raw edges aligned with the lower half of the pillow top, right side down

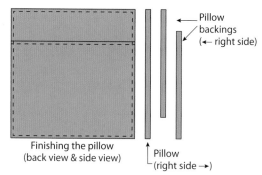

Finishing the pillow
(back view & side view)

Pillow backings
(← right side)

Pillow
(right side →)

With folded edges toward the center, overlap the backing pieces so the raw edges align with the pillow edges.

3 Pin or clip the 3 pieces together. Sew all the way around the square. Trim the corners at an angle. Turn right side out, pushing out the corners with a turning tool. Press.

4 Insert a 16˝ pillow form to finish.

Making the Zippered Pouch

Zippered Pouch, 5¾˝ × 4½˝

1 With the 4˝ × 6˝ piece for the strap, refer to Side Loop (page 45) to make a 1˝ × 6˝ strap. Thread the lobster clasp into the loop and stitch ⅛˝ from the short ends to secure. Stitch again about ½˝ from the loop's fold to hold the lobster clasp in place. Place the raw edges of the strap on the side of an exterior zippered pouch rectangle, about 1˝ below the 6¼˝ edge. Baste in place.

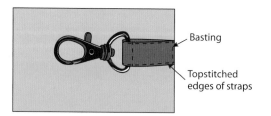

Basting

Topstitched edges of straps

Baste the lobster clasp loop about 1˝ below the top edge.

2 Make a stack in this order from bottom to top, aligning and stitching along the top 6¼˝ side:

+ Zippered pouch exterior, right side up

+ Zipper, right side down

+ Zippered pouch lining, right side down

3 Sew, keeping the zipper pull out of the way while you sew. Press the seams away from the zipper. Fold the exterior and lining pieces wrong sides together.

Repeat this step on the other side of the zipper with the remaining exterior and lining pieces. Press the seams away from the zipper.

4 Unzip the zipper at least halfway. Right sides together, refold the unit to pair the exterior pieces together and the lining pieces together. Finger-press the zipper teeth toward the exterior. Pin or clip the edges together.

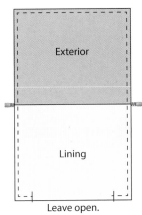

Leave open.

Place the exteriors together and the linings together. Stitch around the perimeter, leaving an opening for turning.

Sew around the perimeter, leaving a 4″ opening in the bottom of the lining. Backstitch at the start and finish. Be sure to keep the strap inside the rectangle as you sew.

5 Turn right side out. Press. Tuck the edges of the opening into the lining and topstitch about 1/16″ from the fold, backstitching at both ends. Push the lining into the pouch and press.

6 Clip the lobster clasp to the D-ring on the pillow's side loop.

Making the Cold Pack

Cold Pack, 6½″ × 5″

1 Pair the 2 muslin rectangles. Stitch around the perimeter, leaving a 3″ gap in a long side. Fill the pouch about ⅔ full with rice; then continue the seam to close the opening.

2 Right sides together, pair the 2 print rectangles. Stitch around the perimeter, leaving a 4″ gap in a long side. Backstitch at the beginning and end of the seam. Turn right side out and push out the corners with a turning tool. Slip the muslin rice pack into the pouch. Tuck the raw edges of the opening into the pouch. Press. Topstitch 1/8″ from the edge around the perimeter.

Book Nook

26″ × 26″ with 20″ pocket

Books and stuffed animals fit neatly in the large pocket and make this item perfect for travel. Pull them out and snuggle up on the pillow for a quiet afternoon of literary bliss.

FABRIC REQUIREMENTS AND CUTTING INSTRUCTIONS

	FABRIC:	FOR:	CUTTING:
❏	9 squares 5″ × 5″ or larger from various prints, or 9 charm squares	Nine-Patch block	From each print, cut 1 square 5″ × 5″.
❏	2 yards black yarn-dyed linen	Nine-Patch block border	Cut 2 rectangles 7″ × 14″. Cut 2 rectangles 4″ × 27″.
		Pocket lining	Cut 1 rectangle 21″ × 27″.
		Pillow front	Cut 1 square 27″ × 27″.
❏	¾ yard batting	Pocket	Cut 1 rectangle 21″ × 27″.
❏	1 yard floral linen print	Pillow back	Cut 2 rectangles 20″ × 27″.
❏	Findings: 26″ × 26″ pillow form		

Making the Book Nook

Seam allowances are ¼″ for patchwork and ½″ for pillow construction, unless otherwise noted.

NINE-PATCH POCKET

1 Arrange the patchwork squares into a 3 × 3 grid. Sew together to make a Nine-Patch block.

Nine-Patch block— Make 1.

2 Sew the 7″ × 14″ linen borders to each side of the block. Sew the 4″ × 27″ linen borders to the top and bottom.

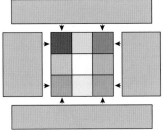

Add borders to the sides first and then to the top and bottom.

3 Right sides together, pair the pocket exterior and the linen pocket lining. Stitch together along a 27″ edge.

Fold the pieces wrong sides together and slip the batting inside. Press. Topstitch ½″ from the seamed edge. Quilt the patchwork as desired.

4 Right sides up, place the pocket at the bottom edge of the pillow top, aligning the raw edges. Baste in place.

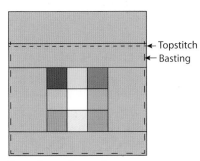

← Topstitch
← Basting

Baste the pocket to the pillow top.

PILLOW ASSEMBLY

1 On each pillow backing rectangle, fold under ¾″ along a 27″ edge. Press. Fold under another ¾″. Press. Topstitch ½″ from the fold.

2 Make a stack in this order from bottom to top:

+ Pillow top, right side up

+ Pillow backing piece, raw edges aligned with the upper half of the pillow top, right side down

+ Pillow backing piece, raw edges aligned with the lower half of the pillow top, right side down

3 Pin or clip the 3 pieces together. Sew ½″ from the edge all the way around the square. Trim the seam to ¼″ and trim the corners at an angle. Turn right side out, pushing out the corners with a turning tool. Press.

Sew ½″ from the edge all the way around the outside of the pillow square to finish the edges.

Sleepy-Time Friend Kit

BUSY GIRL SPEAKS

*Lynne Goldsworthy of Lily's Quilts
(lilysquilts.blogspot.com)*

Any tips for busy people trying to fit sewing into their life? Find a little corner where you don't have to tidy things away every time you stop sewing. I like to have one hand-sewing project that can be picked up whenever I have a free minute.

Organizational tips for the sewing room? I have a trash bin right next to my cutting mat and a scraps box underneath. When I'm cutting, tiny scraps go into the trash, and bigger scraps go straight into the scraps box.

Best advice for a new sewing blogger? Connect with other bloggers. Leave comments on their blogs and respond to their comments on yours. Join online bees, quilt alongs, linky parties, and swaps.

STUFFED DOLL SIZE: *2½″ × 9″*

TOTE BAG SIZE:
6″ wide × 8½″ high × 3″ deep, plus strap

MINI QUILT SIZE: *8″ × 8″*

PILLOW SIZE: *5″ × 3″*

This little stuffed doll can be made into just about any character you like, and his size is a great fit for small hands. Use his pocket for a stuffed friend of his own or special treasures, like jewelry or just-lost teeth. A coordinating tote plus miniature quilt and pillow add extra fun to the mix.

Sleepy-Time Friend Kit

including tote, stuffed doll, mini quilt, and pillow, made with the Goodnight Moon collection from Cloud9 Fabrics.

FABRIC REQUIREMENTS AND CUTTING INSTRUCTIONS

	FABRIC:	FOR:	CUTTING:
☐	Fat quarter navy balloon print	Tote exterior	Cut 2 rectangles 10″ × 11″.
		Optional: Flap closure for tote	Optional: Cut 1 rectangle 4″ × 8″.
☐	Fat quarter yellow mouse print	Tote lining	Cut 2 rectangles 10″ × 11″.
☐	½ yard striped bunny print	Tote exterior pocket	Cut 1 rectangle 10″ × 14″.
		Quilt binding	Cut 1 strip 2½″ × 35″.
☐	½ yard batting	Tote exterior	Cut 2 rectangles 10″ × 11″.
		Tote pocket	Cut 1 rectangle 10″ × 7″.
		Quilt	Cut 1 square 8″ × 8″.
		Optional: Flap closure for tote	Optional: Cut 1 rectangle 3½″ × 3¾″.
☐	¾ yard fusible interfacing (I use Pellon Craft-Fuse.)	Tote lining	Cut 2 rectangles 10″ × 11″.
☐	¼ yard cheater print	Quilt top	Cut 1 square 8″ × 8″.
☐	¼ yard blue cow print	Quilt back	Cut 1 square 8″ × 8″.
☐	Fat eighth white balloon print	Pillow	Cut 1 rectangle 5½″ × 6½″.
☐	⅛ yard navy star print	Stuffed doll body	Cut 2 rectangles 3″ × 4½″.
		Stuffed doll pocket	Cut 1 rectangle 3″ × 8″.
☐	⅛ yard light brown sketch print	Stuffed doll head	Cut 2 rectangles 3″ × 3½″.
		Stuffed doll ears	Cut 4 rectangles 1″ × 3″ for bunny ears.
			Cut 4 squares 1½″ × 1½″ for shorter animal ears, such as those for cats or bears.
☐	Findings: 20″ length of 1″ cotton webbing for tote strap, stuffing, adhesive basting spray; optional: 3″ strip of ¾″ hook-and-loop tape for tote's flap closure, extra-sharp permanent marker or fabric marker		

Making the Friend

Seam allowances are ¼″ unless otherwise noted.

1 Draw the shape of the ears onto the ear rectangles. You can easily make bunny ears by trimming off the top corners of the ear piece to form a point in the middle. Cut out the ears and pair them up into 2 pairs. Sew a scant ¼″ from the outside of the ear shape, leaving the bottom of the ear open. Backstitch at both ends. Carefully turn the ears right side out and press. If you like, you can topstitch just along the ear's edge.

2 Right sides together, pair a head rectangle with a body rectangle. Sew together along a 3″ edge. Repeat with the remaining head and body rectangle. Press seams toward the body.

3 Wrong sides together, fold the pocket rectangle in half to make a pocket 3″ × 4″. Topstitch ¼″ from the fold. Place the pocket on top of a body piece, aligning the raw edges. Baste in place.

Stuffed doll with bunny ears, 2½″ × 9″

4 Draw a curve along the top of the head rectangles and cut along the line.

Trim off to round edges.

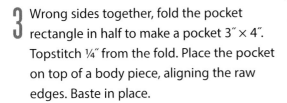

5 Make a stack in this order:

+ Body/head unit, right side up

+ Ears, placed on either side of the head, with the top center of the ears pointing toward the center of the face and the open edges of the ears sticking just slightly above the curve of the head

+ Other body/head piece, right side down

Draw a curve at the top of the head.

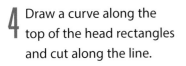
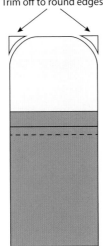

6 Pin or clip the pieces together. Sew around the perimeter of the stuffed doll. Backstitch at both ends. Leave the bottom open for turning.

Ear placement

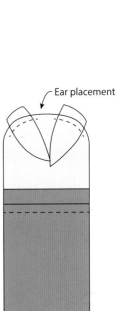

7 Turn the stuffed doll right side out and fill with stuffing. Tuck the bottom raw edges inside the opening and top-stitch ¹⁄₁₆″–⅛″ from the fold.

8 Draw the face with a permanent marker or fabric marker; just be sure to test the fabric first for bleeding!

Point the ears toward the center of the face before you add the other head/body unit.

Making the Tote Bag

Seam allowances are ½˝ unless otherwise noted.

Tote bag, 6˝ wide × 8½˝ high × 2˝ deep, plus strap

1 Use adhesive basting spray to adhere the batting to the wrong side of the exterior bag pieces. Following the manufacturer's instructions, iron the interfacing to the wrong side of the bag lining pieces.

2 Wrong sides together, fold the exterior pocket piece in half to make a rectangle 7˝ × 10˝. Press. Slip the pocket batting inside the fold. Topstitch ¼˝ below the fold.

3 Trim a 1½˝ square out of the lower (10˝ side) corners of both exterior pieces, both lining pieces, and the pocket piece.

4 Baste the pocket in place on the lower end of the bag front, leaving the cut-out squares open.

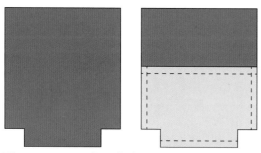

Trim squares away from the bottom corners of the exterior pieces, lining pieces, and pocket. Baste the pocket to the exterior bag fabric.

5 Right sides together, pair the exterior pieces. Sew ½˝ seams on the sides and bottom, leaving the cut-out squares open. Repeat with the lining pieces, but this time leave a 5˝–6˝ opening in the bottom of the lining for turning.

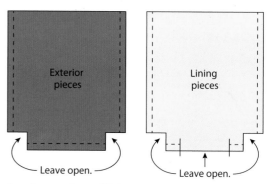

Sew the exterior and lining pieces together.

6 Pinch together the cut-out squares in the bottom of the bag exterior so that the side and bottom seams line up with each other. Sew ½˝ from the edge to box the bottom corners. Repeat with the bag lining pieces.

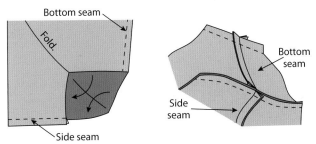

Sew the cut-out edges together to form boxes in the bottom corners.

7 Turn the bag exterior right side out. Center the short ends of the webbing along the side seams of the bag exterior, lining up the short raw ends of the webbing with the top of the bag. Sew ⅛˝ from the ends.

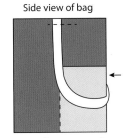

Baste the strap to the bag exterior.

8 Right sides together and aligned at the side seams, place the bag exterior inside the bag lining. Clip or pin the openings together and sew ¼˝ from the top opening.

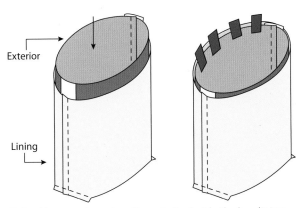

Right sides together, place the exterior inside the bag lining.

9 Turn the bag right side out through the opening in the lining. Use a turning tool to push out the corners. Press.

10 Tuck the raw edges inside the lining gap and press. Topstitch about ¹⁄₁₆˝ from the fold, stitching the gap closed.

11 Push the lining inside the bag. Press. Topstitch ¼˝ from the top edge of the bag.

ADD AN OPTIONAL FLAP CLOSURE

1. Right sides together, fold the flap piece in half so that the short ends meet. Stitch together along each side.

2. Turn the flap right side out. Use a turning tool to push out the corners. Push the batting inside the flap and topstitch ¼″ from the seamed edges.

3. Center the hook-and-loop tape ½″ from the closed end of the flap. Topstitch, just inside the edge, around the perimeter of the strip.

4. Before you sew the exterior pieces together, place the exterior rectangle that does not have the inner pocket sewn to it faceup on the work surface. Center the raw edges of the flap (hook-and-loop tape side up) on the top edge of the exterior rectangle. Baste ⅛″ from the top.

Center the other half of the hook-and-loop tape 1¼″ from the top of the front exterior bag rectangle. Topstitch in place just inside the hook-and-loop tape.

When your bag is done, you'll have a neat closure on top, ready to use!

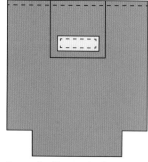

Baste the flap to the bag exterior.

Sleepy-Time Friend Kit made with stuffed kitten "friend" and a coordinating tote with flap. Fabrics are from the Catnap collection by Lizzy House for Andover.

Making the Mini Quilt

1 Make a quilt sandwich in this order from bottom to top:

+ Quilt backing, right side down

+ Batting

+ Cheater print quilt top, right side up

Adhere layers with adhesive basting spray. Quilt as desired.

2 Fold the binding strip in half lengthwise and press. Bind as desired.

 **Bright Idea!**

Instead of using a cheater print, sew nine different 3˝ squares together in a 3 × 3 grid to make a custom quilt for your little friend!

Mini Quilt, 8˝ × 8˝

Making the Pillow

1 Right sides together, fold the pillow fabric in half to make a rectangle 3¼˝ × 5½˝. Using a ¼˝ seam, sew along one long side and one short side, leaving a short side open.

2 Turn the pillow right side out and fill it with stuffing. Tuck the raw edges inside and press. Topstitch ⅛˝ from the edge all the way around the pillow.

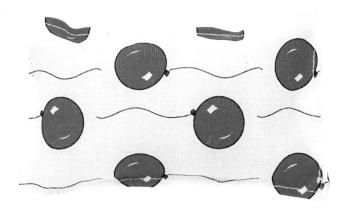

Pillow, 5˝ × 3˝

Baby Love Set

CRAWL PILLOW SIZE: *18″ × 12″*

FLUTTER QUILT SIZE: *37″ × 35″*

This sweet little butterfly quilt and caterpillar pillow welcome the new babies in your life. Colorful prints make these pieces a perfect fit in the nursery. Make one item if you're in a hurry or sew up the complete set if you have the time.

CRAWL PILLOW FABRIC REQUIREMENTS AND CUTTING INSTRUCTIONS

	FABRIC:	FOR:	CUTTING:
☐	Scraps at least 3″ square of 5 different green prints	Caterpillar body	From each of 5 prints, cut 1 square 3″ × 3″.
☐	3″ scrap of black with white dots	Eyes	Cut 2 ovals using pattern (page 63).
☐	⅓ yard white with black dots	Background	Cut 1 rectangle 1½″ × 3″. Cut 1 rectangle 1½″ × 10½″. Cut 2 rectangles 1½″ × 4″. Cut 2 rectangles 3″ × 15″.
☐	⅛ yard purple floral	Border	Cut 1 strip 2½″ × 15″.
☐	⅛ yard pink print	Border	Cut 1 strip 2½″ × 15″.
☐	⅛ yard yellow print	Border	Cut 1 strip 2½″ × 12½″.
☐	⅛ yard blue print	Border	Cut 1 strip 2½″ × 12½″.
☐	½ yard batting	Pillow interior, front and back	Cut 2 rectangles 19″ × 13″.
☐	½ yard muslin	Pillow interior, front and back	Cut 2 rectangles 19″ × 13″.
☐	½ yard green leaf print	Backing	Cut 1 rectangle 19″ × 13½″.
☐	Findings: 1 invisible zipper 20″–22″ long, 1 pillow form 12″ × 18″, adhesive basting spray, fabric gluestick, black thread		

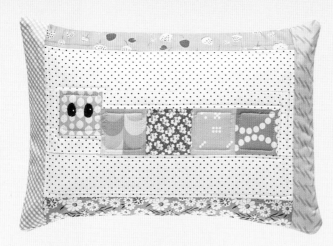

Crawl Pillow

18″ × 12
To brighten any nursery

Making the Pillow

1 Choose a green square for the caterpillar's head. Baste the eyes onto the face with fabric glue. Machine appliqué with black thread and a zigzag stitch. Stitch at least twice around each eye to secure them.

Sew the 1½″ × 3″ background rectangle below the head.

 Add eyes to a green square and sew a background strip to the bottom.

2 Stitch the other 4 green squares together in a long row.

Sew the 1½ × 10½″ background rectangle to the top of the row.

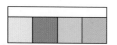 Sew 4 squares together and add a background rectangle to the top of the row.

3 Refer to the Pillow Top Assembly diagram to sew the 1½″ × 4″ background rectangles to the sides of the caterpillar block. Sew the remaining 2 background rectangles to the top and bottom of the block.

4 Sew the purple border to the bottom of the block and the pink border to the top. Sew the blue border to the left side and the yellow border to the right.

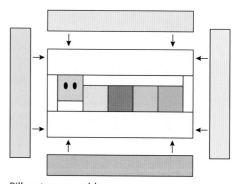

Pillow top assembly

5 With adhesive basting spray, adhere the muslin pieces to the batting pieces. Adhere the pillow top to the batting side of a batting/muslin unit. Quilt as desired.

6 Fold under ½″ on a long edge of the pillow backing piece. Slip the remaining batting/muslin unit under the fold and use adhesive basting spray to adhere it to the backing. Quilt as desired, keeping the folded flap free.

7 Refer to How to Finish a Zippered Pillow (page 108) to assemble the pillow.

Flutter Quilt

37″ × 35″
A welcome gift for any baby

FABRIC REQUIREMENTS AND CUTTING INSTRUCTIONS

	FABRIC:	FOR:	CUTTING:
☐	Fat quarter text print	Wing centers	Cut 4 squares 7″ × 7″.
☐	Fat quarter each of 4 medium/dark prints: green, yellow, purple, and orange	Wings	From each of the 4 prints: Cut 1 rectangle 4″ × 7″. Cut 1 rectangle 4″ × 10½″. Cut 1 square 4½″ × 4½″.
☐	Fat quarter each of 4 light prints: green, yellow, lavender, peach	Wings	From each of the 4 prints: Cut 1 rectangle 4″ × 7″. Cut 1 rectangle 4″ × 10½″.
☐	⅛ yard black dot print	Body	Cut 1 rectangle 2½″ × 20½″.
☐	¾ yard white solid	Background	Cut 4 squares 4½″ × 4½″. Cut 2 rectangles 2½″ × 4″.
		Border	Cut 2 strips 4½″ × 27½″. Cut 2 strips 4½″ × 37½″.
☐	1¼ yards white tree print	Backing	Cut 1 rectangle 40″ by width of fabric.
☐	1¼ yards batting	Quilting	Cut 1 square 40″ × 40″.
☐	½ yard aqua print	Binding	Cut 5 strips 2½″ × width of fabric.

Making the Quilt

Seam allowances are ¼″ unless otherwise noted.

WING BLOCKS

1 Pair each of the 4½″ print squares with a 4½″ white solid square. Refer to Traditional Half-Square Triangles (page 106) to make 2 half-square triangles from each pair. Trim to a 4″ × 4″ square.

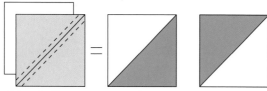

Make 2 half-square triangles from each pair of squares.

2 Sew a 4″ × 7″ dark print rectangle to the right side of the text print square.

3 Sew a half-square triangle to the right side of a 4″ × 7″ light print rectangle. Sew this unit to the top of the unit from Step 2.

4 Sew a 4″ × 10½″ light print rectangle to the left side of the unit from Step 3.

5 Sew a half-square triangle to the left side of a 4″ × 10½″ dark print rectangle. Sew this unit to the bottom of the unit from Step 4.

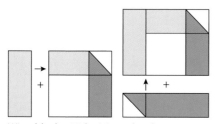

Wing block—Make 1 in each color.

QUILT ASSEMBLY

Refer to the Quilt Assembly diagram.

1 Sew the wing blocks together in pairs on each side.

2 Sew a 2½″ × 4″ background rectangle to each end of the 2½″ × 20½″ body strip.

3 Sew the wing blocks from Step 1 to opposite sides of the unit from Step 2.

4 Sew the 4½″ × 27½″ borders to the right and left sides of the butterfly. Sew the 4½″ × 37½″ borders to the top and bottom.

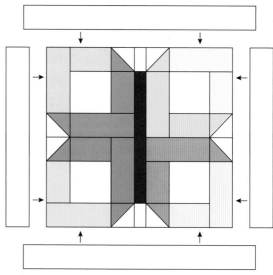

Quilt assembly

FINISHING

1 Layer the quilt backing (right side down), batting, and quilt top (right side up).

2 Quilt and bind as desired.

 **Bright Idea!**

Use the Double-Zip Clutch project (page 34) and a few baby-friendly prints (I used Frolic by Rebekah Ginda for Birch Fabrics.) to sew up a cute diaper pack to go along with the Baby Love Set. Trust me, the new mom will thank you.

Cut 2.

Eye pattern for
Crawl Pillow

Chevron Table Set

TABLE RUNNER
SIZE: *9″ × 37″*

PLACE MAT SIZE:
12″ × 17″

Chevrons are not only a great modern accent on these table items, but they also give you the chance to showcase some of your favorite prints. I chose to use a brown sketch print that has the appearance of linen without the stretchy texture that could make these Flying Geese a little more challenging to sew. One of the place mats is intended for a child, while the other three use the same prints found in the runner.

TABLE RUNNER FABRIC REQUIREMENTS AND CUTTING INSTRUCTIONS

Though the materials list gives you a little leeway for cutting mistakes, you can actually make these chevrons using only a stack of charm squares if you make each cut perfectly!

	FABRIC:	FOR:	CUTTING:
❑	⅝ yard brown print	Flying Geese blocks	Cut 1 rectangle 2½″ × 4½″. Cut 2 squares 2½″ × 2½″.
		Borders	Cut 2 rectangles 3″ × 32½″. Cut 2 rectangles 3″ × 9½″.
		Binding	Cut 3 strips 2½″ × width of fabric.
❑	Scraps at least 5″ square from 15 prints	Flying Geese blocks	From each print: Cut 1 rectangle 2½″ × 4½″. Cut 2 squares 2½″ × 2½″.
❑	½ yard batting	Quilting	Cut 1 rectangle 15″ × 40″.
❑	½ yard floral print	Backing	Cut 1 rectangle 15″ × 40″.

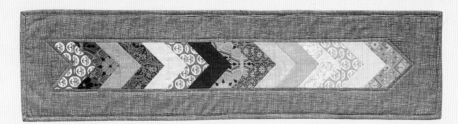

Chevron Table Runner

9″ × 37″, featuring Sketch by Timeless Treasures Fabrics

Making the Table Runner

Seam allowances are ¼″ unless otherwise noted.

FLYING GEESE BLOCKS

1 Arrange the chevron prints (2 squares and 1 rectangle each) in order.

2 Use a pencil to draw a diagonal line from corner to corner on the wrong side of each 2½″ square, including the background squares.

3 To make the first Flying Geese block, start at the top of the chevron. Pair the 2½″ background squares with the top print rectangle.

Right sides together, place a square on the left corner of the rectangle. Sew directly on the diagonal line. Trim the seam allowance to ¼″. Press the brown triangle toward the corner.

Repeat this step with the other brown square on the right side of the rectangle.

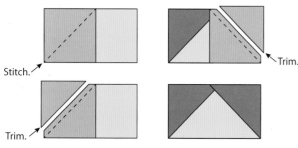

Flying Geese block assembly—Make 15.

4 Repeat Step 3 using the 2½″ squares from the first fabric with the rectangle from the second

fabric in line. Continue making Flying Geese blocks in this fashion. The last block will combine the last 2 print squares with the brown rectangle.

TABLE RUNNER ASSEMBLY

1 Sew the Flying Geese together in 4 groups of 3 and 1 group of 4, and then sew the groups together. This will help keep the rows straight.

Sew together a row of Flying Geese.

2 Sew the 3″ × 32½″ borders to the long sides of the chevron strip. Sew the 3″ × 9½″ borders to the short ends.

FINISHING

1 Layer the backing (right side down), batting, and runner top (right side up).

2 Quilt and bind as desired.

Chevron Place Mats

12″ × 17″

FABRIC REQUIREMENTS AND CUTTING INSTRUCTIONS

Important Note: I've included fabric requirements for one place mat. This way you can easily do the math for the number of place mats that you need. Multiply and enjoy!

	FABRIC:	FOR:	CUTTING:
☐	½ yard brown print	Flying Geese blocks and background	Cut 3 rectangles 2½″ × 4½″. Cut 2 squares 2½″ × 2½″. Cut 1 rectangle 3½″ × 12½″. Cut 1 rectangle 10½″ × 12½″.
		Binding	Cut 2 strips 2½″ × width of fabric.
☐	Scraps at least 5″ square from 3 different prints	Flying Geese blocks	From each of the 3 prints: Cut 1 rectangle 2½″ × 4½″. Cut 2 squares 2½″ × 2½″.
☐	½ yard floral print	Backing	Cut 1 rectangle 13″ × 18″.
☐	Fat quarter batting	Quilting	Cut 1 rectangle 13″ × 18″.

Making the Place Mat

Seam allowances are ¼″ unless otherwise specified.

1 See Making the Table Runner (page 66) for instructions on making the Flying Geese blocks in a chevron pattern.

2 Sew a 2½″ × 4½″ brown rectangle to the top and bottom of the row.

3 Place the chevron row so that the chevrons point up. Sew the 3½″ × 12½″ brown rectangle to the left side of the row and the 10½″ × 12½″ rectangle to the right side.

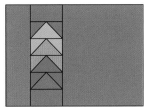

Place mat assembly

4 To finish, trim the place mat to 12½″ × 17½″. Use the same quilting and binding method you used for the runner. (See Finishing, page 66.)

Brass Ring Pillow

PILLOW SIZE: *18″ × 18″*

BLOCK SIZE: *14″ × 14″*

BUSY GIRL SPEAKS

*Angela Pingel of Cut to Pieces
(cuttopieces.blogspot.com)*

Organizational tips for the sewing room? With ever-growing fabric stashes, just keeping fabric organized is key. I wrap my fabric around comic book boards to create a mini bolt; then I store them upright like books. It keeps my space tidy and inspirational.

Best advice for a new sewing blogger? Be true to yourself. Don't try to be another blogger or sewer. Create what moves you, and that will move others.

A traditional Wedding Ring block, also known as a Crown of Thorns block, looks surprisingly modern when transformed into a pillow made of low-volume prints or enlarged to make a lap quilt. "Going for the brass ring" is an old American saying that dates to the turn of the twentieth century, when carousel riders used to reach for brass rings as they straddled horses on the outer ring of the ride. Today the phrase refers to those who are willing to do their utmost to achieve their dreams. It's a lovely thought to accompany a gift for someone special who may be embarking on a new life adventure.

Favorite scraps or charm squares (5″ squares) can be put to use in this miniature version of the original block, embellished with an extra row of piecing on each side. Low-contrast prints and a tight color scheme make a quiet statement with big impact.

Brass Ring Pillow

18″ × 18″, featuring Mercer fabric collection by Dear Stella Design

FABRIC REQUIREMENTS AND CUTTING INSTRUCTIONS

	FABRIC:	FOR:	CUTTING:
☐	Scrap at least 2½″ square from a yellow, peach, or pink novelty print	Center square	Cut 1 square 2½″ × 2½″.
☐	¼ yard gray-and-white polka dot print	Center ring	Cut 4 squares 2½″ × 2½″. Cut 2 squares 3″ × 3″.
		Border	Cut 2 strips 2½″ × 14½″. Cut 2 strips 2½″ × 18½″.
☐	Charm square (5″ × 5″) of the following: • 4 low-volume yellow prints • 4 low-volume peach prints • 4 low-volume pink prints	Half-square triangles	From each of the 12 prints, cut 1 square 3″ × 3″.
☐	30 charm squares featuring at least 20 low-volume black/gray-and-white/cream prints	Half-square triangles	Cut 14 squares 3″ × 3″.
		Squares	Cut 16 squares 2½″ × 2½″.
☐	½ yard batting	Pillow interior, front and back	Cut 2 squares 18″ × 18″.
		Backing	
☐	½ yard muslin	Pillow interior, front and back	Cut 2 squares 18½″ × 18½″.
		Backing	
☐	½ yard low-volume floral print	Backing	Cut 1 rectangle 19″ × 18½″.
☐	Findings: 1 invisible zipper 20″ or longer, adhesive basting spray, 18″ pillow form		

Making the Pillow

Seam allowances are ¼″ unless otherwise noted.

HALF-SQUARE TRIANGLE ASSEMBLY

Right sides together, pair each 3″ black/white/cream print square with a pink, peach, yellow, or gray-and-white polka dot 3″ square. Refer to Traditional Half-Square Triangles (page 106) to make 28 half-square triangles. Trim the blocks to 2½″.

Pair a print square and a neutral square to make 2 half-square triangles. Make 28.

PILLOW TOP ASSEMBLY

1 Arrange the half-square triangles, squares, and center block according to the Block Assembly diagram. You can arrange the colors randomly or make the opposing corners mirror each other.

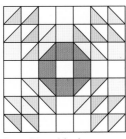

Brass Rings block

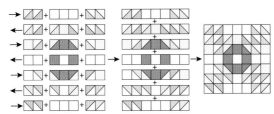

Block assembly

2 Sew the blocks into rows. Sew the rows together.

3 Sew a 2½″ × 14½″ border to opposite sides of the block. Sew a 2½″ × 18½″ border to the top and bottom. Press.

FINISHING

1 Use adhesive basting spray to adhere an 18″ batting square to an 18″ muslin square. Use the spray to adhere the other side of the batting to the wrong side of the pillow top. Quilt as desired.

2 Adhere the remaining batting square and muslin square together. Fold an 18½″ edge of the pillow backing under ½″. Slip the batting/muslin square under the fold, on the wrong side of the backing. Quilt as desired.

3 Assemble the pillow with the backing and a zipper, referring to How to Finish a Zippered Pillow (page 108).

 Bright Idea!

Use random 10″ squares or feature a layer cake of your favorite collection to make finished 9″ half-square triangles for this lap quilt. Leftover blocks can be used to sew up a second quilt, liven up the quilt backing, or create another project.

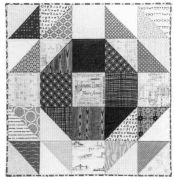

Brass Ring lap quilt, 45″ × 45″
Block size: 9″ square, finished

Envelope Clutch

**MANICURE
KIT SIZE:**
*9½″ × 7″ closed,
9½″ × 17″ open*

ART PACK SIZE:
*15½″ × 12″ closed,
15½″ × 33″ open*

BUSY GIRL SPEAKS

*Kimberly Jolly of The Jolly Jabber
(fatquartershop.blogspot.com)*

Any tips for busy people trying to fit sewing into their life? Wake up 30 minutes early to get some sewing done during the peaceful morning time.

How do you entertain little ones while you sew? My kids have their own fabric cabinet, and I change it up often. They use the scraps to organize their own "quilts" on the floor.

Best advice for a new sewing blogger? Give yourself an achievable goal. Maybe you want to complete a small project each week. Maybe you will post a group of tutorials each month. Also, set boundaries. Many quilters use codenames for their family members just to be safe.

There is lovely simplicity in an envelope clutch. Its classic shape looks both elegant and modern, and the piece can be designed for so many different situations. I've included two sizes that you can easily adapt for a number of uses and occasions.

Manicure Kit

9½″ × 7″ closed, 9½″ × 17″ open

This little clutch is perfect for a manicure set or even a makeup kit. Cheeky novelty prints add a touch of whimsy to the design.

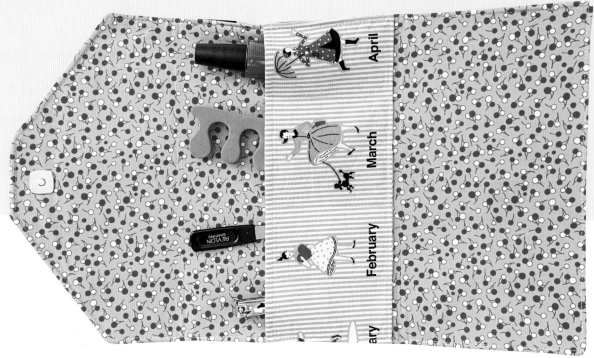

FABRIC REQUIREMENTS AND CUTTING INSTRUCTIONS

	FABRIC:	FOR:	CUTTING:
❑	Fat quarter linen black-and-white novelty print	Clutch exterior	Cut 1 rectangle 10½″ × 18″.
❑	½ yard pink cherries print	Clutch lining	Cut 1 rectangle 10½″ × 18″.
		Pocket lining	Cut 1 rectangle 10½″ × 4½″.
❑	¼ yard green novelty print	Pocket	Cut 1 rectangle 10½″ × 4½″.
❑	⅓ yard heavy sew-in interfacing (I use Pellon 70 Peltex.)	Clutch exterior	Cut 1 rectangle 10½″ × 18″.
❑	½ yard fusible interfacing (I use Pellon Craft-Fuse.)	Clutch lining	Cut 1 rectangle 10½″ × 18″.
		Pocket lining	Cut 1 rectangle 10½″ × 4½″.
❑	Findings: 1 magnetic closure, adhesive basting spray		

Making the Manicure Kit

1 Use adhesive basting spray to adhere the wrong side of the exterior print to the sew-in interfacing. Use an iron to attach the fusible interfacing pieces to the wrong sides of the clutch lining and the pocket print.

2 Right sides together, sew the pocket exterior and lining pieces together along each of the 2 long sides. Turn the pocket piece right side out and press well. Topstitch ¼˝ from the seamed edges.

3 Right sides up, place the pocket on the clutch lining, about 6˝ above the bottom and raw edges aligned at the sides. Baste in place. Stitch ¼˝ from the bottom edge of the pocket to secure it in place. Machine stitch 2 or 3 lines down the main pocket, dividing it into smaller pockets and using measurements that fit the items you plan to place in the clutch. Backstitch at the beginning and end of each line.

4 Follow the manufacturer's instructions to install half of the magnetic closure centered 2⅜˝ from the lower short end of the clutch on the exterior piece. Install the other half centered about 1˝ from the upper end on the lining piece.

5 Right sides together, clip or pin the clutch lining and exterior together, making sure that the magnetic closures are on opposite short ends. On the top end of the unit, use a pencil or fabric marker to mark a point 4˝ from each corner. On each long side, mark another point 3˝ from the upper corner. Cut a straight line between those 2 points on each side, trimming off 2 triangles and making the envelope shape for the clutch flap.

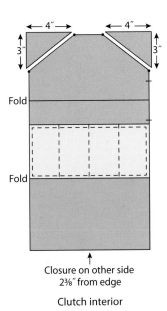

Closure on other side
2⅜˝ from edge

Clutch interior

6 Starting on a long side just above the pocket, sew a ½˝ seam around the perimeter, leaving about a 4˝ gap for turning. Trim the seam to about ¼˝ (except for the opening).

Turn the clutch right side out. Push out the corners with a turning tool. Press. Tuck the raw edges into the opening. Press. Topstitch ⅛˝ from the edge all the way around the clutch.

To close the clutch, fold just below the pocket and about 2¾˝ above the pocket.

Art Pack

15½″ × 12″ closed, 15½″ × 33″ open

The large version of the Envelope Clutch makes a perfect gift for the budding artist in your life. Just add a sketchpad and colored pencils to create a launch pad for creativity.

FABRIC REQUIREMENTS AND CUTTING INSTRUCTIONS

	FABRIC:	FOR:	CUTTING:
☐	1 yard linen novelty print	Exterior	Cut 1 rectangle 16½″ × 34″.
☐	1 yard aqua print	Lining	Cut 1 rectangle 16½″ × 34″.
☐	½ yard text print	Pencil pocket	Cut 1 rectangle 11″ × 16½″.
☐	½ yard herringbone print	Sketchpad pocket	Cut 1 rectangle 12½″ × 18″.
☐	1 yard heavy sew-in interfacing (I use Pellon 70 Peltex.)	Exterior	Cut 1 rectangle 16½″ × 34″.
☐	1½ yards fusible interfacing (I use Pellon Craft-Fuse.)	Lining	Cut 1 rectangle 16½″ × 34″.
		Sketchpad pocket	Cut 1 rectangle 9″ × 12″.
☐	Findings: 5½″ strip of hook-and-loop tape, adhesive basting spray		

Making the Art Pack

1 Use adhesive basting spray to adhere the wrong side of the exterior print to the sew-in interfacing. Use an iron to attach the fusible interfacing to the wrong side of the clutch lining.

2 Right sides together, fold the sketchpad pocket rectangle in half to make a rectangle 12½" × 9". Sew together along each side, leaving the 12½" side open. Turn right side out, pushing out the corners with a turning tool. Slip the pocket interfacing inside the opening and press to fuse. Topstitch ¼" from the folded edge.

3 Using the Clutch Interior Assembly diagram as a guide, place the sketchpad pocket on a long edge of the clutch lining, aligning the raw edges of the pocket with the long edge of the lining. The pocket should be 10¾" from a bottom short end of the clutch. Stitch each side of the pocket ⅛" from the edge, backstitching at the top of the pocket.

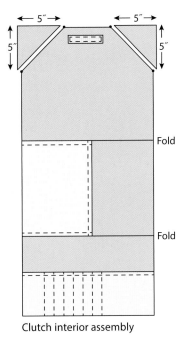

Clutch interior assembly

4 Fold the pencil pocket fabric in half lengthwise, wrong sides together. Press; topstitch ¼" from the fold. Align the raw edges of the pocket with the bottom short end of the clutch lining. Baste in place. Stitch as many straight lines as you need from one long end of the pocket to the other to hold pencils, erasers, or any other art materials. Use the items themselves to help you measure how far apart your lines should be. Be sure to backstitch on each line at the top of the pocket.

5 Center half of the hook-and-loop tape ¼" from the pocket-free edge on the lining side. Topstitch, just inside the edge, around the perimeter of the strip. Center the other half of the hook-and-loop tape about 11" from the other end of the clutch, this time on the exterior side. Topstitch in place.

To close the clutch, fold it on either side of the sketchpad pocket.

6 Right sides together, clip or pin the lining and exterior together. On the top end of the unit, use a pencil or fabric marker to mark a point 5" from each corner. On each long side, mark another point 5" from the corner. Cut a straight line between those 2 points on each side, trimming off 2 triangles and making the envelope shape for the clutch flap.

7 Starting on the long side opposite the sketchpad pocket, sew a ½" seam all the way around the clutch, leaving about a 10" gap for turning. Trim the seam down to about ¼" (except for the opening) and very carefully turn the clutch right side out. Push out the corners with a turning tool. Press. Tuck the raw edges into the opening, press, and topstitch ¼" from the edge all the way around the clutch.

Jet-Set Case

CASE SIZE: *12˝ × 8˝ closed, 12˝ × 18˝ open*

ZIPPERED POUCH SIZE: *8½˝ × 7˝*

Traveling with three little girls in tow is a major event, and the only things that keep me sane are plenty of caffeine and lots of organization. Pretty little cases like this one are just the thing I need for corralling jewelry, makeup, and small toiletry items that might otherwise wander off in the midst of packing. The D-ring loop serves double duty as a closure and as a way to hang the bag when you arrive at your destination.

With a change in fabric choices, the Jet-Set Case can fill a variety of uses. Fill it with school supplies to make a deluxe pencil case. Add sewing materials to make a traveling embroidery or cross-stitch case. The ideas are endless.

Jet-Set Case

Interior, 12″ × 18″, provides plenty of space to carry your most important supplies. My version features the Vintage Happy collection by Lori Holt for Riley Blake Designs.

FABRIC REQUIREMENTS AND CUTTING INSTRUCTIONS

	FABRIC:	FOR:	CUTTING:
❑	½ yard orange stripe print	Case exterior	Cut 1 rectangle 12″ × 18″.
❑	½ yard blue text print	Case lining	Cut 1 rectangle 12″ × 18″.
❑	½ yard heavy sew-in interfacing (I use Pellon 70 Peltex.)	Case exterior	Cut 1 rectangle 12″ × 18″.
❑	¼ yard clear vinyl (I use C&T Publishing's Quilter's Vinyl.)	Vinyl pocket	Cut 1 rectangle 5″ × 12″.
❑	⅛ yard navy iron print	Vinyl pocket binding	Cut 1 strip 2½″ × 12″.
❑	Fat quarter orange hanger print	Zippered pocket exterior	Cut 1 rectangle 8½″ × 12″.
		Zippered pouch lining	Cut 2 rectangles 7½″ × 9″.
❑	Fat quarter white floral print	Zippered pocket lining	Cut 1 rectangle 8½″ × 12″.
❑	Fat quarter navy large floral print	Zippered pouch exterior	Cut 2 rectangles 7½″ × 9″.
❑	¼ yard batting	Zippered pouch	Cut 2 rectangles 7½″ × 9″.
❑	¾ yard twill tape, 1″ wide	Hanging loop	Cut 1 piece 1″ × 5″.
		Wraparound tie	Cut 1 piece 1″ × 18½″.
❑	¼ yard navy small floral print	Binding	Cut 2 strips 2½″ × width of fabric.
❑	Findings: adhesive basting spray, ¾″ hook-and-loop tape, fabric gluestick, zipper 9″ or longer for zippered pouch, zipper 12″ or longer for zippered pocket, 2 D-rings (1″ size)		

Making the Jet-Set Case

VINYL POCKET

1 Use adhesive basting spray to adhere the wrong side of the lining to the heavy sew-in interfacing.

2 Wrong sides together, fold the 2½″ × 12″ pocket binding strip in half lengthwise. Press. Unfold, and then fold the long sides in to meet at the center fold. Press. Fold again at the original line, sandwiching the raw edges inside the strip.

Fold the long edges in to meet at the center fold.

3 Place a long edge of the vinyl inside the folded binding. Topstitch about ⅛″ from the edge of the binding, closest to the vinyl.

4 Place 2 halves (both the same side—furry or scratchy) of hook-and-loop tape on the back of the vinyl pocket binding, 3½″ from each side. Use a fabric gluestick to secure the halves while you topstitch each just inside the edges.

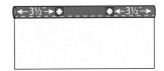

Position hook-and-loop tape 3½″ from each end.

5 Place the other halves of the hook-and-loop tape 3½″ from the sides and 5″ from the short end of the case lining. Topstitch each just inside the edges.

6 Right sides up, align the raw edges of the vinyl pocket with the lower short end of the lining, making sure that the pieces of hook-and-loop tape match. Baste in place.

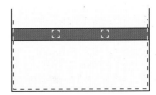

Baste the vinyl pocket onto the lining, matching raw edges and hook-and-loop pieces.

ZIPPERED POCKET

1 Stack in this order from bottom to top, aligning and stitching along a 12″ side:

+ Exterior, right side up

+ Zipper, right side down

+ Lining, right side down

Press the fabric away from the zipper and fold wrong sides together.

2 Repeat Step 1 to attach the lining and exterior to the other side of the zipper. To position the fabrics correctly, fold the lining in half, right sides together, to align the other end of the lining with the other side of the zipper. Repeat with the exterior fabric. It will look as though you have 2 fabric tubes linked together at the zipper.

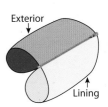

Sew each end of the exterior and lining to opposite sides of the zipper.

3 Turn the pocket right side out. Flatten the tube so that the zipper is in the center. Press.

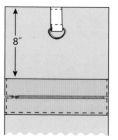

Place the zippered pocket 8″ from the top edge.

Place the pocket on the front of the case lining, 8″ from the top edge of the lining and about ¾″ above the top edge of the vinyl pocket. Sew a scant ¼″ from each side edge. Stitch ⅛″ from the bottom edge of the pocket. Leave the top edge free to be a pocket of its own.

CASE ASSEMBLY

1 Use adhesive basting spray to adhere the case exterior to the opposite side of the heavy sew-in interfacing.

2 Fold the 1″ × 5″ piece of twill tape in half, raw edges together. Thread both D-rings into the loop. Stitch ¾″ from the fold and again ¼″ from the raw ends. With raw edges aligned, center the loop along the top edge of the lining. Baste ⅛″ from the edge.

3 Fold a short end of the 1″ × 18½″ length of twill tape under ¼″ and then another ¼″. Topstitch ⅛″ from the fold. Center the other end of the twill tape at the top of the exterior, opposite from the D-ring loop. Baste ⅛″ from edge.

4 Sew the strips of binding fabric together end to end. Press the long strip in half lengthwise. Bind the outside edge of the case using your favorite binding method.

5 To close the case, fold just below the zippered pocket and about 4″ from the top of the case. Tuck the separate zippered pouch (below) inside the large pocket located behind the zippered pocket. Wrap the long end of twill tape around the outside of the case and thread it through the D-rings to keep the case securely closed.

MAKING THE ZIPPERED POUCH

Zippered Pouch, 8½″ × 7″

1 Use adhesive basting spray to adhere the zippered pouch batting to the wrong side of the zippered pouch exterior rectangles.

2 Refer to Making the Zippered Pouch (page 46) for the First Aid Station to complete the pouch.

Make Something Bigger:

Projects for Time and Travel

I must govern the clock, not be governed by it. —Golda Meir

While there will always be occasions that call for quick projects, it's good to leave room in your life for the occasional challenge. There's going to be a moment when you're browsing online and a new pattern catches your eye. It's gorgeous and interesting, and it already has a growing following among the blogs. Your fingers are itching to get started. "But how," you ask, "am I going to find time for something that big? Small finishes I can do, but that? No way."

All that is about to change.

Splitting a Big Project into Manageable Pieces

As far as I'm concerned, a project is "big" if …

+ It means a lot of hand sewing. This includes projects involving English paper piecing, embroidery, or hand quilting.

+ It's made up of quilt blocks that are difficult to piece or have lots of small pieces.

+ The quilt itself is physically large, calling for a large number of blocks.

This is not a project that will be finished in a day, a weekend, or perhaps a whole month of solid sewing. And even if you tried to crank it out by working on it every day until it was finished, you might be sick to death of it before it's done. Where's the fun in that? It makes more sense to break it down over a longer period of time.

For example, English paper piecing projects have a natural order. First you cut out paper templates—or buy them if you can afford it. Then you choose fabrics, baste to paper, hand stitch the pieces together, and turn them into a finished project. Each step can be assigned to a day, week, or month on your calendar.

Quilting projects that involve a lot of blocks or very complicated blocks also can be divided easily. If you're working on a Christmas quilt that you want to finish by the beginning of December, start working in September or October. Plan to finish one or two blocks every week. Assign a week apiece for assembling the top, making the backing, quilting, and binding. Follow the plan and your quilt should be ready in plenty of time for snuggling beside the Christmas tree.

Whatever your project, study the pattern and break up the steps into manageable bites. Work backward from the finish date, assigning a section to each week. Not only will you find it possible to get the project done in a reasonable amount of time, but you'll also be able to work on it without getting burned out.

You'll need a place to store your project so your workspace is free for the rest of your daily sewing. I like to keep my projects in either plastic drawers—one drawer per project—or in plastic scrapbooking cases. Both are just the right size for quilt blocks, with enough room leftover for the rest of the fabric and notions.

Photo by Heidi Staples

Keeping long-term projects in plastic cases leaves room in your workspace for other projects. I just love this block designed by my friend Kristy Lea.

Traveling with Your Sewing

If you're like me, you have plenty of opportunities to take your sewing on the road. Doctor appointments, lessons for your kids, time spent waiting in the car for your husband to get off work—these are all perfect moments for portable sewing. Having a small project packed and ready to go is a wonderful way to keep your hands and mind busy during what could otherwise be a long stretch of idle time. My favorite on-the-go sewing activity? I love basting and sewing hexagons for projects like the Dotty Hexagon Pillow (page 90). They are small and easy to transport, and you can start and stop at any point without compromising the quality of the project.

If you plan to be out of the house a little longer, say for a weekend getaway or a vacation with family, you can still bring your sewing along if you wish. (By the way, it's okay if you don't wish.) When I travel, I like to bring more than one project with me so that I have options to choose from during my free time. Pack as light as you can—bring along just the basic tools and notions for your project.

Whether you're sewing on the go or on the slow, remember … the point is to enjoy yourself.

Try an on-the-go technique like hexagons or sew a carry-along case (such as the Girl Friday Sewing Case, page 98) for your sewing notions.

Summer Tourist Quilt

QUILT SIZE: *44″ × 44″*

BLOCK SIZE: *12″ finished*

Sewing up one of these quilts is like sitting down after your last vacation to look at all the pictures you took on your trip—oh, the memories! You can use the pieces in your scrap bucket or cut a square from each new print that comes to live on your fabric shelves. *Summer Tourist* is a quilt to be made over time, sewing up a block whenever you have enough prints collected. This is also a great project for using leftover charm squares and mini charm squares.

If you're looking for instant gratification, try something smaller like the *Weekend Tourist* (page 89). This mini quilt is a great way to showcase some of your favorite prints when you're looking for a fun, quick finish.

FABRIC REQUIREMENTS AND CUTTING INSTRUCTIONS

	FABRIC:	FOR:	CUTTING:
☐	Scraps at least 2½″ square from 324 prints, 36 for each of 9 color groups (Choose 18 saturated-color prints and 18 low-volume prints in each color group.)*	36-Patch blocks	From each of the 324 prints, cut 1 square 2½″ × 2½″.
☐	⅞ yard white solid	Sashing and border	Cut 9 strips 2½″ × width of fabric. Subcut 2 strips into 6 strips 2½″ × 12½″. Subcut 4 strips into 4 strips 2½″ × 40½″. Join remaining 3 strips end to end. Subcut 2 strips 2½″ × 44½″.
☐	1½ yards batting	Quilting	Cut 1 square 54″ × 54″.
☐	3 yards black-and-white print	Backing	Make 1 square 54″ × 54″.
	* I chose red, orange, yellow, green, aqua, blue, purple, pink, and gray.		

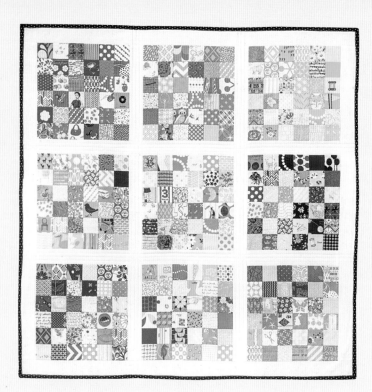

Summer Tourist

44″ × 44″, 12″ blocks

Making the Quilt

36-PATCH BLOCK

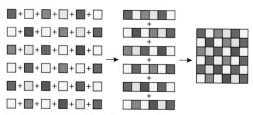

Make a 36-Patch block in each color group, alternating saturated and low-volume prints.

1 Arrange the 36 squares for each color group into a 6 × 6 grid, alternating saturated and low-volume prints. Sew the squares into 6 rows of 6 squares each, pressing each row in alternating directions

2 Sew the 6 rows together to form a 36-Square block.

QUILT ASSEMBLY

1 Arrange the blocks into a 3 × 3 grid. Sew a 2½″ × 12½″ white solid strip between the blocks in each row.

2 Sew a 2½″ × 40½″ strip between each row.

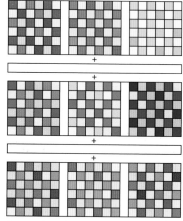

Sew sashing between the blocks in each row and between the columns.

3 Sew a 2½″ × 40½″ border to the top and bottom of the quilt. Sew a 2½″ × 44½″ border to the top and bottom.

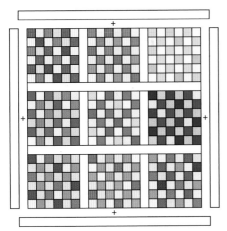

Quilt assembly

WEEKEND TOURIST

To make this lively mini quilt, start with Nine-Patch blocks that finish at 6″. Place the saturated squares at the center and corners of each block and the low-volume prints in between. A text print for the sashing and border adds even more interest.

Weekend Tourist, 18″ × 18″, 6″ blocks

FINISHING

1 Cut the 3-yard piece of black-and-white print in half along the crosswise grain. Trim off the selvages and sew the 2 halves together along the lengthwise grain to make a rectangle 54″ high by twice the width of fabric. Trim to 54″ square.

2 Stack the quilt backing (right side down), batting, and quilt top (right side up). Quilt and bind as desired.

BUSY GIRL SPEAKS

Lindsay Conner of Lindsay Sews (lindsaysews.com) & Craft Buds (craftbuds.com)

Any tips for busy people trying to fit sewing into their life? Late nights are my best time for finishing projects.

Do you have any quick organizational tips for the sewing room? People think it's crazy, but I actually don't own an ironing board; I find that it takes up more space than I'd like. Instead, I covered a cushion in home decor fabric and use that as a portable, tabletop ironing station.

Why did you start blogging? I started as a way to document my own projects and share them with out-of-town family and friends. It motivated me to finish projects, because I couldn't wait to post about them!

Dotty Hexagon Pillow

PILLOW SIZE:
17″ × 12″

Here's your chance to give hexagons a try! Grab a stack of solid-color charm squares and put together this salute to the color spectrum. If you're feeling feisty, try making the pillow with prints instead of solids. Either way it's bound to brighten up your next rainy day.

FABRIC REQUIREMENTS AND CUTTING INSTRUCTIONS

	FABRIC:	FOR:	CUTTING:
☐	5″ charm squares in 44 various solid colors	Hexagons	Trim each charm square to 3¼″ × 3¼″.
☐	Fat quarter of white solid	Hexagons	Cut 15 squares 3¼″ × 3¼″.
☐	½ yard batting	Pillow interior, front	Cut 1 rectangle 18½″ × 13½″.
		Pillow interior, back	Cut 1 rectangle 18½″ × 13½″.
☐	½ yard muslin	Quilting	Cut 2 rectangles 18½″ × 13½″.
☐	½ yard black-and-white print	Pillow back	Cut 1 rectangle 18½″ × 13½″.
☐	Findings: 1 invisible zipper 20″–22″, adhesive basting spray, 1 pillow form 12″ × 18″, 59 paper hexagon templates 1¼″ for basting (Purchase precut or use the pattern, page 93, to copy and cut your own.)		

Dotty Hexagon Pillow

17" × 12", featuring Kona Cotton Solids by Robert Kaufman Fabrics

Making the Pillow

BLOCK ASSEMBLY

If this is your first time with hexagons, be sure to do a little research on basting the hexagons and sewing them together. See Resources (page 111) for links. If you're already a hexie fan, be sure to check out Tacha Bruecher's masterpiece *Hexa-Go-Go* for some incredible project ideas!

1 Baste each trimmed charm square to a 1¼" hexagon paper foundation, using your preferred method.

2 Refer to the Hexagon Assembly diagram to arrange the hexagons into 7 rows, 4 with 8 hexagons each and 3 with 9 hexagons each. Space the white hexagons among the colored ones.

3 Sew the hexagons together into 7 rows. Sew the rows together.

Hexagon assembly

4 Remove the basting threads and hexagon foundations. Press.

5 Use adhesive basting spray to adhere the wrong side of the pillow top to the batting. Adhere muslin to the other side of the batting. Quilt as desired. Trim the final piece to 12½" × 17½".

6 Fold an 18½" side of the backing rectangle under ½". Slip the batting piece for the back under the fold and adhere it to the wrong side of the backing rectangle. Adhere the muslin to the other side of the batting. Topstitch ¼" from the fold to secure it in place. Quilt the backing as desired. Trim the final piece to 12½" × 17½", keeping the folded flap free.

7 Refer to How to Finish a Zippered Pillow (page 108) to assemble the pillow.

WORKING WITH WHITE OR LIGHT HEXAGONS

It can be difficult to use white solids or light prints in hexagon projects, because once you remove the basting papers, there's a round shadow in the middle of each piece that shows where the fabric seam is folded behind the hexagon. You can take care of the problem one of two ways:

1. Use the hexagon pattern to cut hexagons from fusible interfacing such as Pellon's Craft-Fuse. When you remove the paper hexagons from your project, replace them with the interfacing hexagons. Place the fusible side of the interfacing toward the wrong side of the fabric and press in place with an iron.

2. Rather than trim your fabric to a hexagon shape before basting it to paper templates, use a fabric square with at least 1″ of fabric on each side of the hexagon. For this project, I recommend 4½″ squares. The excess fabric may be a little bulkier than you're used to, but the extra seam allowance will cover the entire back of the hexagon and eliminate the shadow completely.

BUSY GIRL SPEAKS

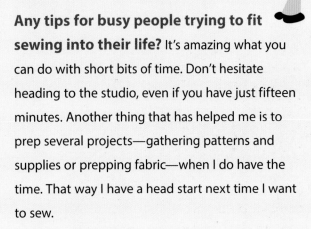

Debbie Jeske of A Quilter's Table (aquilterstable.blogspot.com)

Any tips for busy people trying to fit sewing into their life? It's amazing what you can do with short bits of time. Don't hesitate heading to the studio, even if you have just fifteen minutes. Another thing that has helped me is to prep several projects—gathering patterns and supplies or prepping fabric—when I do have the time. That way I have a head start next time I want to sew.

Any other ideas? I find it much more fun being a "non-monogamous" sewist—having several projects going at once just increases the inspiration for me. If I don't feel like quilting, maybe piecing sounds fun, or maybe cutting out a new project.

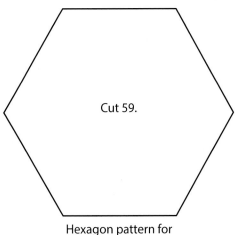

Cut 59.

Hexagon pattern for
Dotty Hexagon Pillow

Starlet Mini Quilt

QUILT SIZE: *28˝ × 28˝*
BLOCK SIZE: *24˝ × 24˝*

I love making a project with giant quilt blocks. It gives me the chance to make something a little more intricate, and it only takes a few blocks to make a good-sized project. One block makes a lovely mini quilt for your wall or table, but don't stop there. Check out Bright Idea! (page 97) for more variations.

FABRIC REQUIREMENTS AND CUTTING INSTRUCTIONS

	FABRIC:	FOR:	CUTTING:
☐	¾ yard white solid	Star background	Cut 4 squares 3½˝ × 3½˝. Cut 4 rectangles 3½˝ × 6½˝. Cut 5 squares 6˝ × 6˝.
		Border	Cut 2 strips 2½˝ × 24˝. Cut 2 strips 2½˝ × 28˝.
☐	⅜ yard red print	Star	Cut 6 squares 6˝ × 6˝. Cut 4 squares 3½˝ × 3½˝. Cut 4 rectangles 3½˝ × 6½˝.
☐	⅜ yard black print	Star	Cut 3 squares 6˝ × 6˝. Cut 4 squares 3½˝ × 3½˝. Cut 4 rectangles 3½˝ × 6½˝.
☐	1 yard batting	Quilting	Cut 1 square 32˝ × 32˝.
☐	1 yard text print	Backing	Cut 1 square 32˝ × 32˝.
☐	½ yard aqua print	Binding	Cut 4 strips 2½˝ × width of fabric.

Starlet Mini Quilt

28″ × 28″

Making the Quilt

BLOCK ASSEMBLY

1 Right sides together, pair the following 6″ squares:

+ 1 pair of white/black

+ 2 pairs of red/black

+ 4 pairs of white/red

2 Refer to Half-Square Triangle Quartet (page 107) to make 4 half-square triangles from each pair of squares, for 28 total. Trim each to 3½″ square.

Make 4 half-square triangles from each pair of squares.

3 Follow the Block Unit Assembly diagram to make 1 center unit, 4 corner units, and 4 side units.

Make 1.

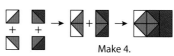

Make 4.

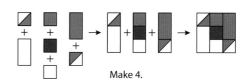

Make 4.

Block unit assembly

4 Arrange the units in a 3 × 3 grid. Sew the blocks together in rows and then sew the rows together.

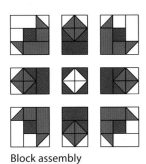

Block assembly

5 Sew the 2½″ × 24″ borders to opposite sides of the block. Sew the 3″ × 30″ borders to the top and bottom.

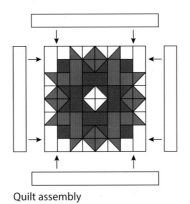

Quilt assembly

Finishing

1 Stack the backing (right side down), batting, and quilt top (right side up).

2 Quilt and bind as desired.

 **Bright Idea!**

Now that you've tried a mini quilt, why not make something bigger? Combine two blocks for a table runner, three to make a decorative accent for the end of your bed, four for a throw quilt, and six or nine to make a complete bed quilt. Just adjust the size of your borders and sashing to get the perfect fit.

Starlet Table Runner, 24″ × 48″, featuring Reminisce by Bonnie Christine for Art Gallery Fabrics

BUSY GIRL SPEAKS

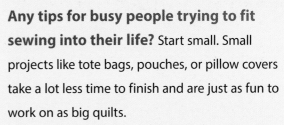

Svetlana Sotak of S.O.T.A.K. Handmade (sotakhandmade.blogspot.com)

Any tips for busy people trying to fit sewing into their life? Start small. Small projects like tote bags, pouches, or pillow covers take a lot less time to finish and are just as fun to work on as big quilts.

Best advice for a new sewing blogger? Make and write about what you love. Do what makes you happy, and it will show through your work. In sewing, as well as blogging, we can sometimes go through "dry periods" when we don't feel like doing either. It's perfectly okay to take a break, do something else, and recharge. When you get back, you'll be fresh and full of new ideas.

Girl Friday Sewing Case

CASE SIZE:
8½″ × 10½″

Back in the 1930s, a "Girl Friday" was another term for your most reliable personal assistant. You'll feel the same way about this little sewing case, which has plenty of room for your next project, along with a handy tool pocket on the front. Get ready to travel in style!

FABRIC REQUIREMENTS AND CUTTING INSTRUCTIONS

	FABRIC:	FOR:	CUTTING:
☐	¼ yard dark print	Pocket exterior	Cut 1 rectangle 6½″ × 9½″.
		Accordion pocket	Cut 1 rectangle 7½″ × 9½″.
☐	Fat quarter medium dotted print	Case exterior	Cut 2 rectangles 9″ × 8¼″.
☐	½ yard light novelty print	Case lining	Cut 2 rectangles 9″ × 11″.
		Pocket lining	Cut 1 rectangle 6½″ × 9½″.
☐	Fat eighth text print	Divided pocket	Cut 1 rectangle 6½″ × 9″.
☐	⅛ yard linen	Case exterior accent	Cut 2 rectangles 9″ × 3¼″.
☐	¼ yard batting	Case exterior and accent	Cut 2 rectangles 9″ × 11″.
☐	¾ yard fusible interfacing (I used Pellon Craft-Fuse.)	Case lining	Cut 2 rectangles 9″ × 11″.
		Divided pocket	Cut 1 rectangle 6½″ × 4½″.
		Front pocket exterior and lining	Cut 2 rectangles 6½″ × 9½″.
		Accordion pocket	Cut 1 rectangle 3¾″ × 5″.
☐	Findings: Button, hair elastic, 2″ length of twill tape for side loop, 9″ or longer zipper, adhesive basting spray		

Girl Friday Sewing Case

8½″ × 10½″

Making the Case

Seam allowances are ¼″ unless otherwise noted.

POCKETS

1 Fuse interfacing to the wrong side of the pocket exterior and pocket lining fabrics.

2 Wrong sides together, press the divided pocket rectangle in half to make a rectangle 6½″ × 4½″. Slip the 4½″ × 6½″ interfacing inside the fold, leaving the ¼″ seam allowance at the bottom free. Fuse in place. Topstitch ¼″ below the fold.

3 Baste the divided pocket in place along the sides and bottom of the pocket lining. Sew a line down the center, back-stitching at both ends, to divide it into 2 pockets.

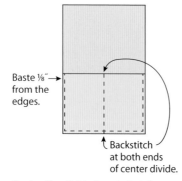

Baste ⅛″ from the edges.

Backstitch at both ends of center divide.

Center the divided pocket at the bottom of the pocket lining.

4 Wrong sides together, press the accordion pocket fabric in half lengthwise to make a rectangle 9½″ × 3¾″. Slip the 3¾″ × 5″ interfacing inside the fold, leaving the ¼″ seam allowance at the bottom free. Fuse in place. Topstitch ¼″ below the fold.

Fold back each side at the interfacing edges. Press. Topstitch ¼″ from each fold, backstitching at both ends. Fold the sides back out so that they extend about ¾″ past the fold line on each side, with a small amount of pocket still folded behind the interfacing. Press with the seams toward the sides. Stack the accordion pocket on top of the divided pocket and lining. Baste ⅛″ from the sides and bottom edge.

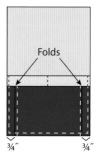

Folds

¾″   ¾″

Make the accordion pocket and baste on top of the pocket lining and divided pocket.

5 Pinch the hair elastic in half and stitch across the center. Stack in this order from bottom to top:

+ Pocket lining, right side up

+ Hair elastic, centered at the top of the lining piece with the loop pointing down

+ Pocket exterior, right side down

Stitch around the perimeter, leaving a 4″ opening on the upper portion of one side for turning. Clip the corners at an angle.

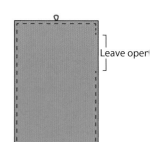

Leave open

Stitch the pocket exterior and lining together.

6 Turn the pocket right side out. Push out the corners with a turning tool. Tuck the raw edges into the opening and press. Topstitch ⅛″ from the edge.

7 Fold the top of the pocket down about 3¼″ to create a flap. Press. Close the flap and mark where the loop touches the front of the accordion pocket. Sew a button to that spot.

Case Assembly

1 Fuse the 9″ × 11″ interfacing to the wrong side of the case lining fabric.

2 Right sides together, sew a case exterior piece and a linen accent piece together along a 9″ side. Repeat with the other case exterior and linen accent. Press the seams open. Use the adhesive basting spray to adhere batting to the wrong side of both. Topstitch the linen accent piece ¼″ from the seam.

3 Wrong sides together and short ends aligned, fold the twill tape in half. Stitch about ⅛″ from the ends. Align the raw edges of the loop about 1″ from the top left, with the left side of an exterior case rectangle about 1″ below the top edge. Baste ⅛″ from the edge.

4 Center the pocket on the top half of the case front, about 1″ from the sides, top, and linen accent. Pin in place.

5 Open the pocket and pin or clip the flap out of the way. Starting at the upper left corner, stitch carefully across the flap fold line, and then stitch ⅛″ from the edge around the perimeter of the pocket. The stitching will trace over the already-existing topstitching on the sides and bottom of the pocket.

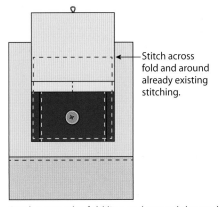

Stitch across fold and around already existing stitching.

Stitch across the fold line and around the pocket.

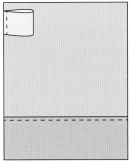
Case front

Case back

Sew a case exterior and accent piece together. Make 2. Baste a twill loop to the left side of the unit that you will use for the case front.

6 Stack in this order, aligning top edges:

+ Case exterior, right side down

+ Lining, right side up

+ Lining, right side down

+ Exterior, right side up

Optional: Use a round object like a cup or bowl to trace and cut rounded corners at the lower edge of each case and lining piece. If you're careful, you can cut them all at once with a rotary cutter.

7 Restack in this order from bottom to top, aligning and stitching along the top 9″ edge (not the linen end of the exterior):

+ Case exterior, right side up

+ Zipper, right side down

+ Case lining, right side down

Use a zipper foot if you prefer. Press the exterior and lining away from the zipper so they are wrong sides together.

8 Repeat Step 7 to stitch the other exterior and lining pieces to the other side of the zipper.

9 Unzip the zipper almost all the way. Right sides together, pair the exterior pieces, being careful to match the linen accent seams. Repeat with the lining pieces. Finger-press the zipper teeth toward the case exterior. Stitch around the perimeter, leaving a 6″ opening on the 9″ end of the lining and backstitching at the start and finish. Clip the corners at an angle.

10 Turn the case right side out. Use a turning tool to push out the corners. Press. Fold the raw edges into the opening in the lining and press. Topstitch across the bottom of the lining to close. Push the lining into the bag and press.

Fill the case with your latest project and hit the road!

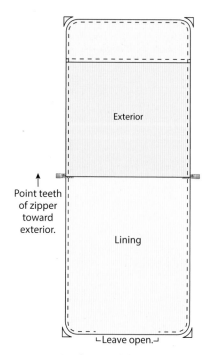

Point teeth of zipper toward exterior.

Exterior

Lining

Leave open.

Stitch around the perimeter of the exterior/lining units.

Joy

Happiness is not a goal ... it's a by-product of a life well lived. —Eleanor Roosevelt

Photo by Heidi Staples

My girls and their quilts

One of my biggest achievements in the past year was to begin teaching my three daughters how to sew. My girls were still pretty young when we got started—just three, four, and six years old—but they had been begging to do this with me for months. I wasn't entirely sure how I was going to make it all work, especially with the many dangers that lurk in the corners of a sewing room. Access to the cutting board was definitely out, and I didn't want them going near the sewing machine unless I was running the show. I finally decided that I would let them have total creative control in the design process and limited participation in the actual sewing.

I spent several days sewing small quilts with my daughters that fall, and now I look back on it as one of the best things I ever did. Every part of the process was an adventure to them. They loved digging through my scrap pile, picking out their favorite colors and prints, figuring out a quilt design, and putting their hands on top of mine as we sewed together. I loved hearing their funny little jokes, holding them close on my lap, and listening to their dreams while we worked together. Their fearlessness as artists took my breath away. They knew exactly what they liked, and they embraced it with arms wide open. There were moments when they were so excited about what we were doing that they would actually start giggling with pure happiness.

I had planned to teach my girls how to sew, but in the end, they taught me. I could explain and demonstrate the mechanics of making a quilt, but they taught me how to sew with abandon, make what I loved, and enjoy every moment of the making. And each time I see one of them snuggling up with the quilt we stitched together, I'm reminded afresh that sewing is not intended to be one more item at the bottom of my daily to-do list. It's meant to be a pleasure. By pouring love and creativity into the works of my hands, I have one more way to bless the people around me and, in the process, be blessed myself.

And that, my friends, is joy.

Sewing Basics

If you are new to sewing and quilting, I encourage you to learn the basic techniques from classes at your local quilt shop or by looking at tutorials online. There are many resources to help you learn how to sew a consistent ¼″ seam, use rotary cutting equipment, layer and baste a quilt, machine or hand quilt, and bind a quilt. See Resources (page 111) for some ideas and a link to C&T Publishing's Quiltmaking Basics.

Supplies

See Resources (page 111) for where to buy the products I use. Here are some items that I try to keep in stock:

+ Quilt batting—I most often use eco-friendly blends from Pellon.

+ Fusible batting—I used to keep this on hand, but now I often use regular batting and adhesive basting spray to achieve the same effect. The choice is up to you.

+ Fusible interfacing—I use Craft-Fuse by Pellon.

+ Heavy sew-in interfacing—I use Peltex 70 by Pellon.

+ Vinyl—I use Quilter's Vinyl by C&T Publishing.

+ Zippers in a wide range of lengths and colors—I always have 9″, 14″, and 24″ lengths, since those can be easily adjusted for a range of project sizes, and white, gray, and cream, since those neutrals go with anything.

+ Bag hardware, including D-rings, lobster clasps, magnetic snaps, ¾″ hook-and-loop tape, and zipper charms

+ Thread—I use Aurifil and Gütermann thread almost exclusively.

+ Buttons

+ Twill tape

+ Cotton webbing

+ Solid-colored linen

+ Linen prints in various styles and colors

+ Cotton prints in various styles and colors

+ Neutral cotton solids, like white and gray

+ Adhesive basting spray

+ Sewing machine needles

It takes a little time to build up your stash, but what a great feeling to have everything you need to make just about anything whenever you want. If you time your purchases with sales at your favorite shops, you can make even better use of your sewing budget. Keep a shopping list just for sewing supplies in your workspace. Update it so you'll be prepared when you get the next online coupon code or sale flyer.

FABRIC

Your fabric stash doesn't have to be enormous. I know people who own a fraction of the fabric that I do and others who collect far more. All manage to make perfectly beautiful projects with what they have. I try to stock a large number of fabrics that will play well with others: dots, stripes, sketchy prints, text prints, solids, and neutrals. Be careful with novelty fabrics, which are the sewing equivalent of trendy fashion choices—you may love it today but wonder what you were thinking later. I try to buy novelty prints only when I have a definite plan for using them.

The biggest fabric lengths are always for the quilt backing—usually four to six yards at a time. I buy two or three yards of neutral solids in cotton or linen at a time since I use them often. Occasionally I splurge on a fat quarter stack or a yard of fabric for a special project. But as a rule, my go-to purchase length is the dependable half-yard. It's large enough to make 95 percent of the projects I would tackle at the last minute, but not so big that it's going to break the bank or eat up all my storage space.

Techniques

You'll find several projects that call for half-square triangles. Here are my two favorite methods for cutting these little beauties . . .

HALF-SQUARE TRIANGLES

Traditional Half-Square Triangles

With this method, you can make two half-square triangles from two squares that are ⅞˝ larger than the finished size of the block. In my instructions, I start with squares that are 1˝ bigger than the finished block size, giving you room to trim them to the perfect size.

1 Right sides together, pair 2 identically sized squares. Use a ruler and a pencil or Hera marker to mark a straight line from one corner to the opposite corner of the top square, dividing it in half on the diagonal.

Draw line.

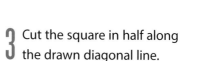

2 Stitch a scant ¼˝ seam on either side of the line.

Sew.

3 Cut the square in half along the drawn diagonal line.

4 Open the 2 resulting squares and press the seam toward the darker fabric. Trim each square to the correct size for your project.

Half-Square Triangle Quartet

With this method, you can make four half-square triangles from just one pair of squares. How easy is that?! The only drawback is that the outer edges of the half-square triangles will be on the bias, so take care with the edges as you trim these and sew them into your project.

1 Right sides together, pair 2 identically sized squares. Sew a ¼˝ seam around the perimeter of the squares.

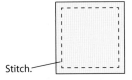

2 Use the ruler and your rotary cutter to cut the squares in half diagonally from corner to corner in both directions.

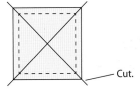

3 Open the four resulting squares and press the seam toward the darker fabric. Trim each square to the correct size for your project. Remember to handle these gently, since you're dealing with bias edges that can stretch!

How to Finish a Zippered Pillow

Several of my pillows are finished with a zipper. Here are the instructions for that process.

1 To accommodate the zipper, I have added ½˝ to the edge of the backing where you will sew the zipper. Use adhesive basting spray to adhere the batting to the wrong side of the backing, leaving the extra ½˝ of backing free at one end. Adhere muslin to the other side of the batting.

2 Fold the extra ½˝ of backing around the batting and muslin. Press.

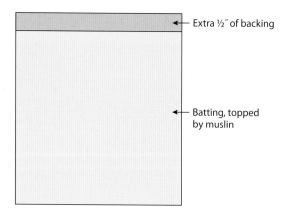

Extra ½˝ of backing

Batting, topped by muslin

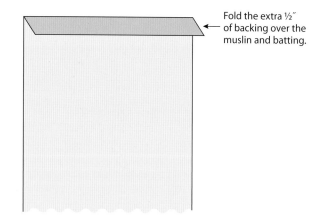

Fold the extra ½˝ of backing over the muslin and batting.

3 Place the zipper, right side down, on top of the pillow top's bottom edge, right side up. Use a zipper foot on your sewing machine to sew the zipper in place ¼˝ from the edge, making sure that the zipper pull is out of the way while you sew.

Press the seam back from the zipper and topstitch ⅛˝ from the zipper on the right side of the pillow top.

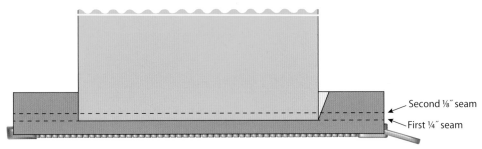

Second ⅛˝ seam

First ¼˝ seam

After you have sewn the zipper onto the pillow top, press the seam away from the zipper and topstitch.

4 Repeat Step 3 on the other side of the zipper with the backing, being sure to match the folded edge of the backing with the zipper.

5 Unzip the zipper at least halfway, but not past the edge of the pillow sides. Pin or clip the pillow top and back right sides together. Switch out your zipper foot for a regular one. Starting at a corner next to the zipper, sew ½˝ around the 3 sides of the pillow, back to the other side of the zipper. Backstitch at least twice at the start and finish.

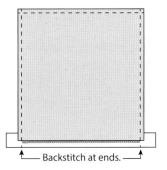

Backstitch at ends.

6 Trim the seam to ¼˝, cutting off the ends of the zipper as well. Turn the pillow right side out, press, and insert your pillow form.

Glossary of Terms

BACKSTITCH: straight stitching in reverse a few stitches to make sure that your sewing holds securely

BASTE: using a long straight stitch to temporarily fasten pieces together, usually with ⅛″ seams

CHEATER PRINT: a fabric print designed to look like pieced quilt squares

CLEAN SWEEP: a short amount of time (five to twenty minutes) spent cleaning your workspace (See Keep Your Work Area Clean, page 19.)

FABRIC AUDITION: testing out a mix of fabrics to see if they look good together as a group (See Hold Regular Fabric Auditions, page 20.)

FINISHED SIZE: the size of a block, not including seam allowance (Usually, this is ½″ smaller than the size of the block before it is assembled into the quilt or other project.)

PROJECT BAG: a plastic bag stocked with supplies for making a specific project (See Be Prepared with Project Bags, page 22.)

STASH: your collection of sewing resources, usually referring specifically to your fabric

SUBCUT: taking a piece that you just cut and cutting it into smaller pieces

TOPSTITCH: machine stitching, usually near an edge or fold and usually for decorative purposes

TURNING TOOL: a blunt, pencil-sized instrument used to push out corners after turning (Alex Anderson's 4-in-1 Essential Sewing Tool includes a turning tool plus seam ripper, stiletto, and pressing tool—very handy! In a pinch, you can also use a chopstick for the same purpose. See Resources, page 111.)

TUTORIAL: a (usually free) pattern or step-by-step explanation of a process

BUSY GIRL SPEAKS
Maureen Cracknell of Maureen Cracknell Handmade (maureencracknellhandmade.blogspot.com)

Any tips for busy people trying to fit sewing into their life? My favorite time to sew is in the late evening, when all the kids are asleep. It's become my favorite way to end the day!

Any ideas for entertaining little ones while you sew? Having craft and art supplies for the kids to use while I sew has been so helpful.

Best advice for a new sewing blogger? Take nice photos of your finished work. There is so much that goes into making each thing, and I love to honor that hard work by showcasing each finish as beautifully and thoughtfully as I can.

Resources

The first place to go for information and products is your local quilt shop. If that is not possible or they cannot help you, then try the Internet for information.

Sewing Basics

BOOKS
Hexa-Go-Go by Tacha Bruecher
ctpub.com

There are amazing online resources. Here are some great places to start:

TIPS & TECHNIQUES FROM C&T PUBLISHING
ctpub.com/quilting-sewing-tips
At the bottom of the page, look for Quiltmaking Basics and Sewing Tips under Support. You can download this section to your own computer or look up a specific topic by clicking on one of the article titles.

QUILTING ARTICLES FROM CRAFTSY
craftsy.com/articles/quilting

HEXAGONS
craftsy.com/article/english-paper-piecing

Sewing Notions

ALEX ANDERSON'S 4-IN-1 ESSENTIAL SEWING TOOL
ctpub.com/notions

AURIFIL THREADS
aurifil.com

GÜTERMANN THREAD
gutermann.com

CLOVER REGULAR WONDER CLIPS
clover-usa.com > Products > Sewing and Quilting > Accessories

Interfacing and Batting

PELLON
Pellon 70 Peltex Ultra-Firm Sew-In Stabilizer
Pellon 808 Craft-Fuse
Pellon Nature's Touch 100% Eco-Cotton Batting or Legacy Eco-Cotton Blend Batting
pellonprojects.com

C&T PUBLISHING
fast2fuse interfacing
ctpub.com/interfacing
Premium Clear Vinyl
ctpub.com/vinyl

Fabrics

NOTE: Fabrics used in the projects shown may not be currently available, as fabric manufacturers keep most fabrics in print for only a short time.

ANDOVER FABRICS
andoverfabrics.com

ART GALLERY FABRICS
artgalleryfabrics.com

BIRCH ORGANIC FABRIC
birchfabrics.com

CLOUD9 FABRICS
cloud9fabrics.com

DEAR STELLA
dearstelladesign.com

RILEY BLAKE DESIGNS
rileyblakedesigns.com

ROBERT KAUFMAN FABRICS
robertkaufman.com

SPOONFLOWER
spoonflower.com

TIMELESS TREASURES
ttfabrics.com

About the *Author*

Photo by James Staples

HEIDI STAPLES spent nine years as a fifth-grade teacher and one as a school administrator before becoming a full-time mom in 2009. Two years of changing diapers and chasing three little girls around the house convinced her that she needed a hobby, and in the fall of 2011, she sewed her first quilt. It quickly led to a full-blown fabric addiction and an ongoing parade of handmade projects. Heidi lives with her husband, three daughters, two parents, and three neurotic dogs in sunny Southern California. You can follow her sewing misadventures on her blog Fabric Mutt at fabricmutt.blogspot.com.